Ralph Ciampa

HEALING THE

SPIRIT

Stories of
Transformation

D1384495

"A remarkable study . . . a work of faith and love . . . yet objectivity and openness of spiritual healing in the lives of people within the mainstream church and synagogue. . . . A real breakthrough that deserves the attention of clergy and people of faith."

—Rev. Dr. Gilbert W. Bowen
Presbyterian Minister, Sr. Pastor
The Kenilworth Union Church
Kenilworth, Illinois

"Dr. McKay and Mr. Musil's project is complementary to the work of the Religious Experience Research Centre. . . . I found not only their efficiency, but also their sympathetic style of working an important aspect of their research. It was a pleasure to have face-to-face contact and an ongoing relationship with such able and enterprising researchers."

—Peggy Morgan, M.A.
Director, The Alister Hardy Religious
Experience Research Centre
Westminster College, Oxford, England

"Healing the Spirit: Stories of Transformation . . . draws one into deeper awareness of God's healing presence each and every moment of our lives. The story of how the Spiritual Healing Project got off the ground, as well as the book's conclusions, are just as important as the stories themselves. I was glad to see that God's healing knows no denominational divisions."

—Rev. Michael Hack, Pastor
Infant Jesus of Prague Parish
Flossmoor, Illinois

HEALING THE

SPIRIT

Stories of
Transformation

Reverend Bobbie McKay, Ph.D.,
and Lewis A. Musil

ThomasMore®

Allen, Texas

ACKNOWLEDGMENTS

We would like to express our thanks and gratitude to the
following people for their invaluable help and support:

Our children and grandchildren
The New Church Community
Reverend Dr. Paul Sherry
Dr. Loretta M. Richardson
Reverend Dr. Gilbert Bowen
Reverend Elizabeth Andrews
The Kenilworth Union Church

John Shea
Dr. Dolores Nicosia
Peggy Morgan, M.A.
Rabbi Mark Shapiro
Rabbi Douglas Kohn
Sandy Krebs
T. Tolbert Chisum
Reverend Wayne F. Prist

The participating congregations
and clergy in the Spiritual Healing Project

Dr. McKay and Mr. Musil can be reached through
the M/M Foundation, P.O. Box 656, Wilmette, IL 60091;
or
you can visit their web site, Bethlehem2.com.

Cover design: Melody Loggins
Interior design: Cami Travis-Groves

Send all inquiries to:

Telephone: 877-275-4725 / 972-390-6300

Fax: 800-688-8356 / 972-390-6560

THOMAS MORE PUBLISHING
200 East Bethany Drive
Allen, Texas 75002-3804

Printed in the United States of America

Library of Congress Catalog Number 00133316

ISBN 0-88347-465-4

1 2 3 4 5   04 03 02 01 00

To God,
who turns out to be the story

"Healing the Spirit *is a book of transformation. It speaks with grace, integrity, power, and joy to the spiritual healing that accompanies the awakening sense of God's presence in all our lives. The personal stories of spiritual healing of so many people from so many differing backgrounds and places are both moving and renewing. To read these stories is to have one's own spirit healed. That certainly was true for me and I am sure will be true for many others as well.*"

—The Reverend Paul Sherry, Ph.D.
Former president
United Church of Christ

"*This remarkable, faithful couple has been on a Spirit-led journey, and they share with us wonderful gifts gathered in the process: stories of God's presence or action in people's lives, moments of transformation, and a vocabulary for us to use in speaking of these experiences to one another. Graced intersections of the everyday and the eternal abound— and there is power in naming them aloud in the presence of others. How amazing, how liberating, how fitting—if our churches could once again become 'safe places' where these experiences can be told and validated!*"

—The Reverend Elizabeth B. Andrews
The Kenilworth Union Church
Kenilworth, Illinois

"*Dr. Bobbie McKay and Lewis Musil have uncovered God's secrets and blessed joy in their quest to find the truth about the healing spirit. Neither gender, race, education, religion, nor position can stop God's grace for all mankind. Travel with Bobbie and Lew as they witness their incredible journey into the churches, temples, and synagogues and come face to face with the healing spirit.*"

—T. Tolbert Chisum
Businessman and philanthropist
Kenilworth, Illinois

CONTENTS

Part I—In the Beginning

Part II—Words, Lessons and Stories

Part III—What We've Learned and What You Can Do

ON CLIMBING TREES, DRINKING FROM THE WATER OF LIFE, AND THE NATURE OF SPIRIT

AS I READ Bobbie McKay and Lew Musil's captivating account of their Spiritual Healing Project, *Healing the Spirit,* I was reminded of climbing trees, the water of life, and the nature of Spirit.

Climbing Trees. My spiritual director came to visit me at the place where I was staying. There were many trees on the property and, as we walked around, she asked, "You climb any of these trees, Jack?"

I had not climbed a tree since I was ten. And I was no good at it then.

"Not on your life," I said.

Then she found a tree whose branches were low to the ground, quickly moved up it, and sat on one of the branches. From her perch in the nook of the tree, she looked around, repeating over and over again, "Now, this is interesting. This is interesting."

In her own teaching-by-example way, she was giving me a piece of spiritual advice. I was living in a magnificent forest, among beautiful trees. But all I was doing was looking at them.

I stepped back and gawked, a distanced observer. This may be the scientific way of knowing, but it does not get you into the inner world of trees. From her spiritual perspective you know things by entering into them and seeing from their perspective. Knowing is not an act of stepping back, but stepping into. It is not an act of disengagement, but of communion. Sitting in the branches of the tree is the only way to know it.

I remembered this teaching when I read the personal and engaged way Bobbie and Lew went about trying to understand spiritual healing in the lives of people. Bobbie began with her own experience and asked if it resonated with anyone else. Most of the world raised their hands.

Their storytelling sessions became a community of people listening to one another and entering into each other's experience. The reality of spiritual healing will not be known by uninvolved observers. Listen with openness to the stories of this book, allow this listening to spur your own memory and recall your own experiences, and tell them to a friend. If you do this, you will have an intuitive sense of what spiritual healing is—and you may be surprised that you are no stranger to it.

The Water of Life. The water of life, wishing to make itself known on the face of the earth, bubbled up in an artesian well and flowed without effort or limit. People came to drink of the magic water and were nourished by it, since it was so clean and pure and invigorating. But humankind was not content to leave things in this Edenic state. Gradually, they began to fence the well, charge admission, claim ownership of the property around it, make elaborate laws as to who could come to the well, put locks on the gates. Soon the well was the property of the powerful and the elite.

The water was angry and offended; it stopped flowing and began to bubble up in another place. The people who owned the property around the first well were so engrossed in their power systems and ownership that they did not notice that the water had vanished. They continued selling the nonexistent water; and few people noticed that the true power was gone. But some dissatisfied people searched with great courage and found the new artesian well. Soon that well was under the control of the property owners, and the same fate overtook it. The spring took itself to yet another place—and this has been going on throughout history.

This story details the fate of the flowing water of the earth in the hands of possessiveness and greed. This water is the type that Isaac of Nineveh talked about: "There is a love like a stream, which dries up when it doesn't rain. But there is a love that is like a mighty spring gushing up out of the earth; it keeps flowing forever and is inexhaustible." This water flows through every country but, unfortunately, each country tries to claim it as its own. The water is just there, freely invigorating all who drink from it. But people do not want to freely receive it, they want to own it and control it. This attempt to seize Spirit forces it to retreat. However, it does not completely disappear. Rather, it moves on, making itself available in another place. This story has often been applied to the various religions and their attempt to control divine grace.

One of the hallmark findings of the Spiritual Healing Project is that Spirit is available to all who know how to open to it. It lives beyond institutions and their guardians. The way to find out where the water is bubbling up is simply to ask people. That is what Lew and Bobbie did. And people told them where the water was and how to drink from it.

11

Rev. Bobbie McKay, Ph.D., and Lewis A. Musil, M.A.

The Nature of Spirit. People who look deeply into the phenomenon of healing usually espouse some type of dimensional understanding of the human. We are people with physical, mental, social, and spiritual capacities. These dimensions interact with one another, but they also have their own laws and operations. For example, the social can influence the spiritual, but it does not work exactly like the spiritual. Or the spiritual can affect the mental, but the mental and the spiritual are not the same realities and do not function the same way. In other words, both the distinctiveness of each dimension as well as their ability to influence one another are recognized.

However, it usually stops there. The understanding is not pushed further. It seems to be enough to assert we are an integrated unity of body, mind, relationships, and spirit. But spiritual traditions go further. They have developed theories about how these various dimensions interlock and interact with one another. The foundation of these theories is the nature of Spirit.

The soul is the deepest center of the person, the ultimate locus of identity, and, metaphorically, has two eyes. The right eye peers into the eternal and the left eye peers into the temporal. This means the soul is a boundary reality, connecting us on one hand to God and on the other hand to our mind-body organism and through that organism to the entire mental and material universe. The trick is to keep both eyes open, but to open the right eye first. When the soul opens to God, it immediately receives Spirit, for the nature of God is to give Spirit. The soul then channels this abundance of Spirit into mind, body, and world. The effect of this flowing Spirit is healing.

In this sense, Spirit does not heal itself, it heals what it touches. As Spirit flows into mind, it brings peace and forgiveness. As Spirit flows through mind into body, it activates the healthy capacities of the body. As Spirit flows through soul and mind-body into world, it strives to hold together the social dynamics that so easily break apart. Spirit is a reality that can be in other realities and not displace anything of those realities. So when Spirit is in mind, mind is elevated. When Spirit is in body, body is elevated. This is just a detailed working out of the medieval theological maxim: grace perfects and elevates nature.

The many stories of spiritual healing in this book cannot be captured in a single formula. However, in all the particular tales I thought I heard echoes of this Spirit-soul-mind-body-world pattern. In the deepest part of themselves (the soul) people turned to God (The Giver of Spirit) and received Spirit that had beneficial effects on their minds, bodies, and relationships. Of course, the beneficial effects cannot be predicted or controlled. Spirit is a resource on its own terms. All we can do is open, and allow Spirit to expand the mind in wonder and gratitude. Which is how your mind will be expanded as you read this book.

John Shea

Advocate Senior Scholar-in-Residence
Park Ridge Center for the Study of Health, Faith, and Ethics

Research Professor
Institute of Pastoral Studies,
Loyola University of Chicago

INTRODUCTION

WHAT IS THE MEANING OF SPIRITUAL HEALING, SPECIFICALLY FOR PEOPLE IN RELIGIOUS COMMUNITIES

HEALING THE SPIRIT: Stories of Transformation is the story of the Spiritual Healing Project: a national study on the subject of spiritual healing, designed and conducted by my husband and myself. The words "project" or "study" suggest an intellectual process of discovery and prediction, and indeed the "Spiritual Healing Project" started out as a research study to discover the meaning of spiritual healing for people in the church. But its ending turned out to be quite a different thing altogether. One does not expect to find miracles and mysteries in the midst of objective data.

We began our study with a simple question: What is the meaning of spiritual healing, specifically for people in the church? In all the recent talk about spiritual healing among the medical and mental health professionals, no one seemed to be raising the issue of spiritual healing in the church, a place where one might expect the subject to be of vital concern. We chose to pursue the answer to that question in the United Church of Christ (U.C.C.), a Protestant denomination of sixty-one hundred churches, rich in ethnic diversity and geographically located across the United States. This is the denomination to which I am connected as a minister. But more importantly, this particular denomination contains a remarkably eclectic population which could uniquely supply the answer to our question. It was a good place to begin. Later on, we would be moved to expand the project, in a way we had never imagined, to include Catholic and Jewish congregations.

We visited 101 U.C.C. churches around the United States from April 1996 to April 1998, and met with over two thousand people who told us literally hundreds of personal stories about spiritual healing. Additionally, most of them filled out a nine-page questionnaire about the subject. So we do have a significant amount of data to be analyzed and discussed about a subject that attracted a lot of attention wherever we went.

Right from the beginning, this project transcended all the words and language we could think of to describe what we were doing. Though technically correct, the words "Spiritual Healing Project" were simply inadequate to the task. They felt like flat, black-and-white objects in a world that exploded with color and multidimensionality. The experience of actually doing the project, talking to over two thousand people about the action of God in their lives, felt like a mystery that kept unfolding, purposefully moving us along a path that was clear and unmistakable. This project belonged to God from start to finish. We were only the vehicles to keep the project in motion; to make the necessary arrangements for travel; to schedule meetings and to hear and carefully record the stories that were shared by our participants. The rest was handled entirely by God's grace and God's instructions.

If that sounds strange, crazy, or at the very least hubristic, all I can tell you is that our experience with the Spiritual Healing Project has created in us such a deep and indelible sense of humility and gratitude for the mystery of God's gifts and presence that all we can do, all we want to do, is to try to share what we have learned and to express our thanks for this amazing experience.

While we started out on a quest to answer a simple question, our study became a mission of faith and a gift of immeasurable value. In each church we visited, with each story we heard, we became more and more aware of the presence of God, not only in the lives of those who participated in the study, but also in the actual meeting itself. The project became infused with the presence of God and suddenly, quite unexpectedly, our lives began to change. As the project came to life, so also did we. We began to experience a renewed spirituality that has become central to our existence. In simply listening to people talking about their experiences of spiritual healing, we felt a deep sense of healing within us. Spiritual healing had become contagious!

Because we didn't set out to "discover" miracles, what happened to us personally became yet another mystery in a long list of experiences that could only be described as wondrous, remarkable, and marvelous. We were no longer engaged in a spiritual healing project. Instead, we were traveling with God and we were finding unmistakable evidence of the unceasing activity of God everywhere we went.

In sharing this amazing experience with us, your life also can become transformed into a spiritual adventure with God as your companion. All it takes is your willingness to open your eyes and ears and heart to the gift of God's presence in your life.

But first, come back with us to the beginning of the project and let us show you how it happened for us. Let us share with you the miracles that unfolded as we discovered just how active God really is in this world. Finally, we will tell you of the unexpected events that occurred just as we thought our project was ending: another one of God's surprises and a fitting ending that turned out to be a brand-new beginning!

PART I
IN THE BEGINNING

CHAPTER I. THE MYSTERY BEGINS

It was an uneventful day. My kids were napping, and I was using the time to get the house clean. Nothing unusual about that. I hadn't been thinking about anything religious—far from it. I'm not sure I was thinking at all. I was just cleaning in that sort of automatic-pilot way of getting done what needed doing. So when it happened, it was a total surprise!

I was dusting some books and one of them just happened to be a Bible. Now, I wasn't a Bible reader so it was more a dust collector than anything else. But on this particular day, I found myself opening the Bible and turning the pages. It didn't feel like I was looking for something as much as following some sort of directive.

When I got to the opening of the Gospel of John, I stopped. Don't ask me why. I just stopped looking and started reading. I read the opening lines once, then a second time, and when I read them a third time, I knew I was changed. My world seemed to stop for a millisecond. Then something in me shifted gears, almost like a course correction, and I felt like I was picked up and set down in a brand-new universe. I knew I was different, even though nothing around me had changed at all. I was still holding the same dust cloth, looking at the same passage in the Bible. But I was changed. It was as if a switch had been turned on and my faith had come to life.

It didn't feel crazy at all. It felt like something had happened that had already changed my life irrevocably. I had no idea what that would mean for me or my family. I didn't know how to talk about what happened. I just know that my life was permanently changed in one moment, on one day when I was least expecting anything to happen.

Later, as I tried to keep up with all the changes in my life, I would have the courage to name this mysterious experience as God acting in my life, bringing me into a new life. It's hard to find the right words. It was a gift, beyond all other gifts, and it has never stopped growing.

HISTORY often calls us to look for a starting point, a moment in time in which something was activated and change occurred. Clearly a wonderful idea to think about, but tough to accomplish. Our multiple-track lives make discernment more a process than an exact science. But if pressed to state precisely when the Spiritual Healing Project first took shape in my mind, I would have answered with a list of dates. In 1994, I began to think about spiritual healing; in 1995, I presented a proposal to the Board for Homeland Ministries of the United Church of Christ to conduct a national study about spiritual healing, using a random sample of churches in the United Church of Christ as the research population for the project. In 1996, my husband and I began to visit our sample of 101 churches, and in 1998 we completed our data gathering in the United Church of Christ.

Yet lists of dates don't begin to touch the reality of the Spiritual Healing Project. They are the facts in an amazing journey, the benchmarks of a process that has occupied most of our waking hours for almost six years. But they don't capture the heart of an experience which was to change both of our lives. They can't tell the story.

Perhaps the project had its earliest roots in 1964 when I experienced a powerful conversion experience which moved me from being an "ordinary housewife with three children and one dog" to becoming a composer, an ordained minister in the United Church of Christ, a licensed clinical psychologist, a writer, and a public speaker. But then I'd have to wonder what precipitated my conversion experience, what prepared the way for the mystery of change that entered my life, unsought and unplanned. Can we ever really pinpoint the exact *beginning* of change?

Clearly, we are not privy to all the actions of God which create new beginnings, strange turns, and sometimes mysterious new directions in our lives. These God connections are born in us at some point in our journey through time, and they are shaped and nurtured until they emerge at what appears to be precisely the right moment. We are made ready by unseen and loving hands and then offered countless opportunities to enter new worlds of understanding, faith, and action.

If we are willing to turn our lives over to these God connections and actions, we enter a spiritual path destined to bring us to the place where we belong and to the reality of God's wish to be fully involved in our lives. But God is highly democratic when attempting to enter our lives. God is the great initiator; the choice to engage in this process of connection is always ours. We have the final vote.

In the early 1990s, almost thirty years after my conversion experience, God planted another seed in my consciousness.

Rev. Bobbie McKay, Ph.D., and Lewis A. Musil, M.A.

Working now as a psychologist and a pastor, I was in the healing "business" for most of the hours of my life. When wearing my psychologist's hat, people came to my office questioning all the complexities of their lives. They shared their pain, wept their losses, and cried out their angers and frustrations. Their suffering felt so senseless and isolating. Does life have to be this way? What can I do to feel better? When will "it" get better? Will "it" get better? Why do I have to suffer and feel so alone? Where is God in all of this?

When acting as a pastor, people raised the same questions about life and about God, except that for church people God sometimes seems even more elusive and remote than in a clinical setting. If God is not here in the church, then where *is* God? What am I doing wrong? I'm at the end of my rope and I've come to the place where God is supposed to be. If I can't reach God here, then I'm out of options. It's hopeless, or perhaps more accurately, "I'm hopeless."

In the midst of these painful sharings, I always sensed God's presence and I knew that the healing process was in God's hands, not mine. As a psychologist, my job was to listen carefully and to be an advocate of the change process. People have a built-in capacity for change and growth if given the opportunity to speak and be heard. Later, I would learn that my real job was to look for God in the healing process and acknowledge the mystery of God's presence to those engaged in the process.

Eventually, I would begin to raise questions about my own conversion experience in the light of the experiences of others. Was my conversion experience a common one? Did other people share the same experience of powerful change as I had? What was the healing process all about? Did it happen suddenly, as my conversion had occurred, seemingly appearing full blown with no preparation? Or is the healing process one of unfolding change, nurtured by a patient and loving God who wants only to be connected to us? What facilitates this healing process? Can we create it or, more importantly, can we make it work faster?!

Psychology could provide some answers. But it could not really bring God into the healing process because the grace-filled work of God is at God's invitation and is not in our control. The first task in the healing process may be to clear out some of the awful emotional debris that overwhelms so many, a job that psychology is well equipped to do. But after that is accomplished, the real task is to look for God's presence in the healing process and to acknowledge God's invitation to become the focus of our lives. Spiritual healing brings us into a new reality that is deep, profound, and God centered.

Then the questions that were to lead to the Spiritual Healing Project began to emerge from some inner place within me, unsought and unannounced. "What if . . ." (always a dangerous beginning); "I wonder what would happen if . . ." (a sure sign of something growing); "I'm really interested in what other people have to say about their spiritual experiences" (the creative process is taking shape); Why not simply ask other people about spiritual healing; what the words mean to them? What has happened in their lives that they would call spiritual healing? How comfortable are they in talking about the subject of "spiritual healing"? In that simple process of inquiry, hidden in those unassuming questions lay the seeds for the Spiritual Healing Project. *The miracle of creation had occurred!*

The "Word," that inner idea, dream, question, curiosity, had taken on a life of its own and was now a new creation, ready to grow and develop. The seed, planted by God and nurtured through whatever experiences were necessary to provide shelter

21

and understanding, had grown sufficiently to move from internal supports into external reality. Small as this seed was, only a series of questions and an idea, it was now undeniably moving out of its internal and safe environment and preparing to go out into the world. The silence of my inner musings and questions needed to come to life in the form of words shared with another. I needed to let someone else know of the miracle that had just occurred.

The choice was simple. I needed to tell my loving and understanding husband what had been growing in my heart and mind. I knew he would listen to my halting and uncertain words without judgment and that he would not think I was crazy, a critically important piece at this delicate stage in the project's development. I also was confident of his willingness to move in whatever direction God would take us. His commitment to a spiritual life was as strong as mine.

Even so, it is uncomfortable and unsettling to put that which grows deep within us as an idea or a dream into the words that transform it from private safety to public scrutiny. Quick judgments or assessments can destroy that which is tender and scarcely able to breathe on its own. It needs the nurturing of love and acceptance and the hope of possibility and it needs to be named as surely as any newborn needs to be identified as unique and separate from every other. This was a loving gift from a Creator God who once again wished to become a part of our God-created world. And the name that we gave the gift was the "Spiritual Healing Project"; an awesome title for a gift that had just survived the creative journey from my soul into the blinding brightness of reality.

It was the first miracle in a journey of two thousand miracles!

CHAPTER 2. THE MYSTERY CONTINUES TO UNFOLD

We were in the basement where my daughter had wisely arranged an office and a playroom. So when she had work to do, the kids would be right there playing. It was comfortable and easy. One day, when I was baby-sitting my grand-daughter, we pulled up a couple of chairs next to the computer and she showed me all the amazing skills that kids today have when it comes to computers. She outdid me for sure, and she was only six years old. But in the midst of her demonstrating her prowess with that complicated machine, she reached over and, without saying a word, she took my hand and simply held it. We stayed in silent, hand-holding communication for what may have been just a few moments. But it was like an eternity of connection in one tiny package of time. No words were necessary. Only the touch of people who loved each other.

I think God is like that ... always reaching out to hold our hand, without words, but with the mystery and simplicity of love and connection and healing.

IMMEDIATELY after the project became an acknowledged part of our lives, the actual shape and form of the project came to life as well. It was a wondrously simple plan, as God is wont to do, especially when we give God the control and stop muddying the operation with our own ideas and plans. (An activity which is much easier to do when you don't have any idea what you're supposed to do anyway!)

I knew we would have to approach the denomination with a specific proposal and a plan. That felt like climbing a tower of rules and procedures that was not going to be easy. Proposal writing is a profoundly complicated operation for those who engage in it regularly. For a novice as I was, the process became a six-month adventure in officially attempting to put what felt like mystery and miracle into proposal form and language!

At first, our understanding of God's plan was modest. Pick out about twenty-five churches that are ethnically, socioeconomically, and geographically representative of the United Church of Christ. Visit them and ask the people directly what the words "spiritual healing" mean to them. Listen to their responses, their words and stories; let them teach you about their experiences. Write a questionnaire so you have a written as well as spoken response to your questions about spiritual healing. It will also give people who don't like to talk in public an opportunity to add their understanding to the study.

In no time, the rest of the plan emerged, uncomplicated and uncluttered. Don't try to learn about spiritual healing in advance. Don't present theories or speculations of others about healing. Let the people in the church who have lived out the mystery of God's presence and love in their lives teach you and direct you. Absorb their words and stories; write them down lovingly and carefully because they are special gifts to be cherished and remembered. Let it be known that all people are welcome to participate: those who choose to share and those who simply come to listen.

The only information we would present had to do with the general nature of spiritual healing. We would invite people to look at this issue in the broadest of contexts. Spiritual healing *can* occur when there is an experience of "curing": when the disease disappears and health returns with no medical explanation. Spiritual healing can also occur when there is *no* "cure," but when people experience a sense of being "healed spiritually." Spiritual healing can also happen when there is no disease, but where a sense of healing is experienced. In other words, if "curing" is our only measure for spiritual healing, then we will miss those countless opportunities in which God's loving actions are present in ways not manifested as physical "cures."

Finally, in the midst of this unfolding of instruction and purpose, we knew one additional fact. If we were to accomplish God's plan as we understood it, we needed to maintain the purity and simplicity of the project, and not subject it to possible changes and alterations that the denomination might impose. The only way to accomplish that was to finance the entire study ourselves. Asking for funding and financial support creates an open door to the needs and agendas of others. Complications and compromises inevitably arise. The plan that had come to life was fully formed and ready to be put into motion. There could be no compromising of the plan and commitment that had already been made.

So on the one hand, we had two miracles in place: the idea and the form. On the other, we now had to convince an institution that needed facts, projections, reasons, and justifications that we had a worthy quest to pursue. Mystery did not seem sufficient cause to convince a hierarchical body that this plan had merit. Even paying for the project ourselves could stir the suspicions of those questioning our agenda and motives.

Other questions challenged the veracity of the project. Was anyone really interested in spiritual healing? Without knowing who we were, would any church be willing to have us visit to talk about spiritual healing? Who would come to talk with us? Would they have anything to say about spiritual healing? How would we get a random sample that would be representative of the denomination? Would our data be meaningful?

The official responses to most of these questions were not encouraging. "People really aren't interested in talking about spiritual healing.""We just don't do that around here—that's too 'high church'," or sometimes, "That sounds too weird or too religious." The best advice we received was "to invite a lot of churches to participate if you hope to get even a few to let you in." We were surprised, but not daunted. Having lived the miracle of the project, it was unthinkable not to pursue what we felt was a clear mandate from God

A carefully crafted proposal was submitted to the denomination in September 1995. Two months later, the Spiritual Healing Project was endorsed as presented: no changes, no restrictions, no exceptions. We were ready to take a massive leap into the unknown, fed by the conviction that God was fully in charge of the entire plan. The Spiritual Healing Project was moving into the world and it felt like another miracle had just taken place.

Now the study moved into high gear. But what had already transpired would seem like child's play compared to the problem that now faced us. How *would* we locate a random population of churches that would be ethnically, socioeconomically, and geographically representative of the sixty-one hundred churches in the United Church of Christ? Looking at the book that listed all the churches in the denomination was like facing the climbing of Mount Everest with no experience and no equipment. How do you break down a task of such proportions and produce a sample that has any validity?

The only guideline that we had determined early on for ourselves was one of anonymity. We would not visit a church where either one of us was known. This would allow the results of the study to evolve from the direct experiences of its participants, not contaminated by any association with us or with our ideas.

Once again, God deftly reentered the scene and solved our problem. We received some assistance from a staff member; we gained more help from friends acquainted with churches and pastors in other parts of the country. But mostly we relied on a prayerful process which somehow enabled us to choose a random sample of one hundred churches that turned out to be almost perfectly representative of that ecclesiastical body called the United Church of Christ.

We chose large and small churches; city, suburban, and rural churches; African American, Native American, Hispanic and Philippine churches; a gay community; thriving churches and dying churches; multistaff and single-pastor churches; rich and poor churches; bilingual churches; a multidenominational church housing seven different Protestant denominations; churches serving the needs of changing and mixed neighborhoods; a church in the heart of a heroin district trying to save souls and the city. Our churches spanned the entire United States: from Washington State to Texas to Maine to Florida with all points in between.

We knew our random sample was another gift of God's grace

and presence. There was simply no other explanation for the richness of our sample. With almost no assistance from others, and with no preconceptions as to where we might go with the project, we were now ready to take this show on the road. God had chosen our list of churches, but now we had to invite them to participate in this project. We had to find out if anyone was interested in spiritual healing. We were at a point of no return!

With courage in hand, and never doubting that *someone* would say "yes" to our invitation to come and talk about spiritual healing, a letter was mailed to our one hundred chosen churches in January 1996, asking them to participate in a national study on spiritual healing, presented by strangers, not experts, about a subject that was frankly religious in nature. It was an invitation to engage in *spiritual intimacy*, a process as old as time, but filled with the awesome potential of unknown gifts and rewards for those who would risk the adventure. It was a giant step from the first moment of conception in 1994 and it felt like light-years had passed since those early awakenings.

We stood, holding our breath, poised as if we were on the precipice of an odyssey that would take us away from the familiar and the safe into something that could only be described as God's territory: unknown and yet deeply familiar.

The letters were mailed and we waited.

CHAPTER 3. ON OUR WAY

Before she began to talk, her eyes filled with tears, which moved slowly down her cheeks. She nodded her head as if to give herself permission to tell her powerful story. "I worked in a small bank and one day, a few years ago, several men came in to rob the bank. They blindfolded me and tied me up along with the rest of the employees. I was terrified. I didn't know if any of us would survive. But in the middle of that overwhelming fear, I suddenly felt a sense of peace that seemed to take over my whole being. Nothing had changed in the situation, but I somehow knew we would all be okay. The peace did not leave. And it turned out we were all okay. I knew that was the presence of God. I knew God was there taking care of us. I'll never forget it."

✢ ✢ ✢

WE WROTE A simple letter describing our project and listing the three questions we would raise:

1. What is spiritual healing? What are the *words* you use to describe spiritual healing, in order that we might create a new vocabulary, a language of words that people might use to describe the experience of spiritual healing?

2. What *stories* do you tell about your experiences of spiritual healing, according to your own definition of spiritual healing? What stories are shared in your family, your neighborhood, your church which have to do with spiritual healing?
3. What would a church be like where people were encouraged to talk about spiritual healing?

The questions were part of the God-given package that continued to unfold for us. Their simplicity focused the project into words and stories, those fundamental ways of looking at life and at God, and they brought God's presence immediately into the project. The letter then described who we were, without suggesting that we had expertise in spiritual healing. Finally, the letter offered the necessary endorsement that acknowledged the authenticity of the project. We were official now and the rest was clearly in God's hands, as it had been from the beginning.

In two years time, we had followed our dream to the place where it now stopped. Now it was our turn to watch and wait. Would the gift we were offering be received? Would our mission be allowed to continue? In the days that followed the mailing of the letter, it was as if we were suspended in time, trying to comprehend the mystery we had already experienced. God seemed everywhere: visible, tangible, available, and as close as the word we were waiting for, the "Yes" we hoped to receive.

And the "yes's" came! Ninety-six of our one hundred churches said "yes." "Yes, we are interested in spiritual healing." "Yes, you can come to visit us." "Yes, you can talk with us about spiritual healing." "Yes, you are welcome." Some said, "How soon can you come?" Others asked, "How long can you stay?"

Of the four churches who turned us down, two said they were in the midst of a time of internal struggle; no time for strangers. The remaining two had interesting reasons for refusal. One said they didn't talk about spiritual matters in their church! The other said they were far too intellectual to talk about spiritual matters. But we rejoiced with the 96 percent favorable response that assured us that God's work in the project would continue.

Subsequently, we invited six more churches to participate in the project, churches that would add even more validity to our random sampling. All six churches said yes immediately. Our total was now 102 churches. Sadly, a pastor in one of our churches became critically ill. The time was not right for this community to be talking about spiritual healing. And so we closed our sample at 101 churches, a number four times our original estimate!

Only momentarily did we think about eliminating some churches, making the sample more manageable. The costs were going to greatly exceed any budget we might have had for the project. The commitment to visit all these churches would require considerable time and energy in an already busy schedule; my patients would have to deal with time compromises in our clinical work. Our children would also experience less of our availability and support, though that was less a problem with all of them well into adulthood by now.

But the choice was clear for both of us. What else was there to say? If God had given us 101 churches, then this would be our sample. We were not alone in this journey. We both took a deep breath and then we said the "yes" that was ours to pronounce. Yes, we are committed to this project. Yes, we will visit all the churches in our sample. Yes, we will open our hearts and minds to whatever God had to offer us through this amazing gift we had received.

In all the "yes's" that surrounded us, we knew that we were in the presence of grace and truth. Whatever the journey would teach us, we were ready to learn. Wherever the journey would take us, we were eager and ready to go. The response to our gift had come with a generosity of spirit and enthusiasm and the Spiritual Healing Project was now a reality.

Charged with a new energy and excitement, we were on our way, committed to a journey that had no known destination, but that would permanently change the course of each of our lives.

CHAPTER 4. ON THE ROAD WITH GOD

My grandson was only two years old, but he carried that marvelous wisdom that only the very young possess. We were in my office where he loved to play. It was a special place of paper and pencils, files and drawers—a magic place for this energetic bundle of pure energy. On this particular day, he looked at me solemnly and declared that we had a brand-new game to play. We sat on the floor together and I asked him what the name of our new game would be. "Mom and Dad" was his immediate answer. When I looked puzzled, he said, "I'll show you." Then he demonstrated his wonderful creation.

He would pick up an object in the room and bring it to me while I sat on the floor. My job was to "ooh and aah" over each gift, thanking him for the pleasure of his choice and telling him what a wonderful gift it was. It was enough that I treasured each gift, nothing more. In those few moments of time, we devoted ourselves exclusively to giving and receiving.

Each time we played "Mom and Dad," the room became a holy place, a place filled with love and peace. I can't explain it. It just happened.

Rev. Bobbie McKay, Ph.D., and Lewis A. Musil, M.A.

AS I FACED the reality of actually starting the project, I realized I had never planned what we would do when we visited our churches. The stage was set, of course, for the next gift. Ordinarily, I make meticulous preparations for any presentation I make. It makes me feel less nervous which makes a more enjoyable and informative experience for everyone. But as I approached the occasion of the first Spiritual Healing Project, I found myself making no plans—and not feeling nervous, experiencing instead a remarkable combination of letting go and trusting that something would happen. And indeed it did.

It was Saturday, April 20, 1996, 9:30 A.M. We arrived at our first church with questionnaires in hand and paper to take down words and stories. A group of about twenty interested looking people awaited our arrival; an assortment of breakfast treats were attractively arranged on a table; the pastor greeted us and then trustfully turned the meeting over to me and to whatever was going to happen. I took a deep breath, looked around at those expectant faces, and turned the whole thing over to God. The words came effortlessly as I told them how the project had come into being. Then I raised the first question we had come to ask.

"What are the words that you use when you think about spiritual healing? What words do you associate to the experience of spiritual healing? We need a vocabulary of words to help people talk about spiritual healing. Will you help us?" The responses came immediately and these same words would be repeated one hundred more times as the official opening to each presentation of the project:

Spiritual healing talks about having a relationship with God.
Spiritual healing talks about change and transformation.
Spiritual healing talks about hitting bottom; things getting worse before they get better.

Spiritual healing talks about confusion and then clarity.
Spiritual healing talks about letting go of my control.
Spiritual healing is a conversion experience.
Spiritual healing is always a surprise, an unplanned-for event.

In the time that followed, we heard at least a dozen remarkable stories of healing, told with tears, triumph, pain, joy, each story yielding to the next with no silence in between. It was as if we had turned on a switch that released a flood of memories and moments in which God became present within each of these shared experiences. We had already determined that my husband would write down the stories while I encouraged the storyteller to provide whatever details were necessary. But there was scarcely time to record one story before the next was already in progress.

Ninety minutes later, when the pace of the stories was slowing down, we prayed together, acknowledging the gift of God's actions in the lives of so many people and the sharing of these experiences. We sensed a powerful need to praise God and to express our gratitude for God's healing presence. Questionnaires were filled out; we hugged our new friends and went out in the blazing April sun, awestruck with the gifts we had just received.

The Spiritual Healing Project had begun its journey of 101 churches. The response we had received was so rich and so remarkable that we drove in amazed silence as we headed for our next church, three hundred miles away. Each moment, each story seemed like another gift in our growing collection of miraculous moments. We planted this first experience in a garden of experiences to come, an unforgettable array of breathtaking color and life.

After our first church experience, a format for the presentation of the project gracefully emerged and formed the fabric for each subsequent experience. God's loving plan was direct, simple, and always successful. We prayed together at the beginning of our time together to acknowledge that God was indeed with us. Scripture about healing, carefully read for each group, gave us our spiritual foundation and anchored us within Jesus' healing ministry. Those words, deeply familiar to everyone, were about to come to life in the twentieth century.

> *And Jesus went about all Galilee, teaching in their synagogues, and preaching the gospel of the kingdom, and healing all manner of sickness and all manner of disease among the people.* (MATTHEW 4:23)

> *And when he called unto him his twelve disciples, he gave them power against unclean spirits, to cast them out, and to heal all manner of sickness and all manner of disease.* (MATTHEW 10:1)

> *The Spirit of the Lord is upon me, because he hath anointed me to preach the gospel to the poor; he hath sent me to heal the broken-hearted, to preach deliverance to the captives, and recovering of sight to the blind, and to set at liberty them that are bruised.* (LUKE 4:18)

As I invited people to pronounce the words that defined spiritual healing for them, I would first share some of the words we heard from our first church as a way to stimulate their thinking process. But it took very little encouragement for people to eagerly share the words that defined spiritual healing for them. Later, as we turned toward stories, we found the same immediacy of response. People could scarcely contain their stories about God's love and presence in their lives. It was as if they were engulfed in a flood that had to have expression. As the number of churches increased, so did our catalogue of stories, captured on paper and lovingly held in our hearts as constant reminders of the wonder of our experience.

The gift of the format seemed almost mystical in its ability to open people to the experience of sharing their spiritual lives from a depth seldom experienced in a one-time-only meeting. So many people would say to us: "I've never told this story before to anyone"; or "I've waited twenty (or thirty) years to tell this story"; or "I've never felt I could tell this story in church. "We were receiving a continuous flow of unforgettable treasures, gifts to savor and cherish.

Finally, before the questionnaires were handed out, we would pray a second time to acknowledge our gratitude for the grace of God and for our time together. This prayer, coming after our shared words and stories, was so filled with the presence of God that it was always accompanied by tears. The tears held the truth that indeed God had been with us. Hand in hand, in a circle of healing, we felt an intimacy of spirituality that transcended all of our differences. We had discovered a place where all are welcome and equally loved by a Creator God who chooses to be with us and to share in all that life presents to us.

The final gift of the format we used in each church came very early in our travels. We ourselves had an experience that captured the essence of our work and, in its simplicity, it spoke to the entire reason we were doing the project. It didn't happen in a church; in fact, the setting could hardly be called religious or spiritual. But the message we received carried the truth of the project and it came from the world's most unexpected source.

We were traveling between Philadelphia and Baltimore on Highway 95, a road that works its way south, providing an expedient route if you don't mind the bumps and cracks. But it also houses those gifts of the highway—the oases that provide us with food, gas, coffee, Mrs. Field's cookies—and a variety of maps.

We stopped, bought our required cookies and coffee, and then stopped to get a map of Baltimore. We had four churches to visit in the Baltimore area, and we were running on a very tight schedule. The map man stood behind the counter—a nondescript older fellow, who seemed pretty uninvolved with the whole operation. No one else was around at the time and so I thought we could accomplish our task quickly. I approached him and said in a friendly tone, "I'd like a map of Baltimore, please."

He said, "What for?" punctuating his words with a rather peculiar attitude of wonder and surprise.

I said, "Because we're going to Baltimore," my voice betraying some impatience with the question. We didn't have time for this.

He responded in a louder voice, with an even more challenging question, "What for?"

I was getting annoyed by this time, concerned about our tight schedule, and responded with a definite edge of hostility in my voice.

"Because we're bringing a Spiritual Healing Project to four churches in Baltimore!" (I might just as well have added, "So there!" But I didn't.)

Without a pause, he spoke three statements that carried a message of absolute truth:

"Spiritual healing happens all the time. And it's happening right here with the three of us talking. And I feel better!"

And we felt like we had experienced a miracle on Highway 95. In three short sentences, he had defined our project and had spoken to the heart and soul of what we would learn from every church we visited. We would share that story with all our remaining churches. It touched everyone, reaching across all boundaries, and it spoke directly to the reality that we do feel better when we acknowledge the presence of God in our lives. It's that simple.

We had indeed come home to the place where we belonged. We were now in God's Territory, where everything is a gift from God. Six months later, we stopped once again at the oasis on Highway 95, eager to reconnect with this stranger who had spoken such wisdom to us. We wanted to render the thanks and gratitude we were too stunned to produce on our earlier visit. As you might suspect, our original map man was nowhere to be found. A rational explanation might suggest that he was sick, or retired, or simply on vacation. But our project had taught us that the gift was there when we needed it and that was sufficient. We were content with wherever or whoever he was.

We visited our final Protestant church in April 1998. We had begun our project in an African American Church; we ended our project at a Native American Church. It felt fitting to encompass all the diversity we had experienced within these two powerful healing traditions. Like marvelous bookends, they reminded us of the depth of our experience, the wonder of what we had learned and the unforgettable gifts we had received. We hung a large map in our home with all the cities we had visited marked with large black dots so we could visually appreciate the length and depth of our journey. We had traveled the entire United States, and visited with over two thousand people. Our lives were profoundly and permanently changed.

In retrospect, we wondered just how we had done it! How did we find the time, energy, money? How did we make the plane schedules, find the roads, locate the churches in areas we had never visited before? How did we accomplish this while we were both still working full-time at other jobs? But we also knew that we didn't "do" it alone. Without God's continued presence and support, we would never have accomplished this profound journey. That support was also reflected in the responses from each of our churches along the way and in the ongoing support and interest of friends and family.

We were finished, but only with the first stage in our project. Now would come the challenge to translate our experience into words and to try to bring the story of the project to life for others. How else to do that but to tell our story and to share the words and stories we had heard, letting the whole experience speak of the mystery and meaning of God's healing presence in all of our lives.

In the summer of 1998, filled with love and gratitude, we first began to write this book. Our lives were so changed by this time that we were eager to bring our experience to any who would read and listen. We felt a deep sense of satisfaction and contentment. We had accomplished our goal and it exceeded any hopes or any expectations we could have imagined. We thought we were finished . . . and then . . . God paid us another visit!

Once again, God's entry was quiet, not insistent, scarcely noticeable except for the persistence of the idea being presented. It wouldn't go away. It began innocently enough with a fascinating lecture on Scripture and story, presented by a Catholic theologian John Shea who enchanted us with his message. At first, we simply absorbed the lecture and felt enriched by what we had learned. But then the idea started to make itself known around the edges of our consciousness. At first, it seemed ridiculous, farfetched, impossible. We couldn't do that . . . no, it would never work . . . not feasible . . . definitely not!

But God persisted, and we did that human process called

"wondering." Could we . . . would it be possible for us . . . do you think it could happen that we might take the Spiritual Healing Project into the Catholic church? The words were out and our response was immediate. We stopped writing our book.

Miraculously, doors opened to admit two amazed and dazzled Protestants into the heart of the Catholic system. We were invited to present the Spiritual Healing Project to eleven Catholic churches in the Chicago area, specifically chosen to reflect the ethnic and socioeconomic diversity we had achieved in our original study. To say we were grateful for this new turn of events scarcely describes our state of shock. We were in awe, overwhelmed by the generous gift we had been given and humbled by the mystery of God's interventions in our lives. This was a path we would never have taken. And yet, here we were, once again saying "yes." Yes, we get the message. Yes, we will go where you lead us. The door opened and we entered a brand-new world, feeling deeply privileged to participate in such a rich, spiritual tradition.

We began visiting our Catholic churches in the fall of 1998, and completed the last of our churches in April 1999. We presented the project with no changes, replicating exactly what we had done 101 times before. But this time, we had no expectations of what might happen or how we would be received. History reminded us of struggles and strong animosities between Catholics and Protestants, still operating in parts of the world. We were mindful that times have changed and some tensions have diminished. But we understood that we were in unfamiliar territory, inviting a spiritual intimacy that some might not be willing to share with outsiders.

Yet in the first Catholic church we visited, barriers disappeared in the first few moments of our meeting when one of the participants shared the tears that were clear evidence of our common pain, our common humanity. We are so alike! We struggle with the same problems, the same hopes and dreams, the same successes and losses. We all share the same need for God's healing presence in our lives. We are one fabric, with endless patterns of color and complexity. The barriers that separate us are instantly removed when we engage in the process we had come to know so well: the sharing of words and stories about spiritual healing.

Our experience in the Catholic church has convinced us of the universality of the experience of spiritual healing. God's healing presence is a reality which we all share. We had always heard this truth. Now we knew it in a way that transcended understanding because we had lived it. And now, we could finish our book!

Or so we thought. In the fall of 1999, we were gently prompted (by you know who) to realize the obvious fact that the Christian tradition proceeds from the rich heritage of the Jewish tradition. After all, Jesus was a Jew and the early church began in the Jewish community. Our work would be incomplete without pursuing the roots of our faith.

Once again the question of how we could do this was immediately answered by a friend's reminder of a Rabbi I had worked with twenty five years ago. We were fortunate enough to find him at the same Reform Temple and he gave us another incredible "yes." Yes, he was interested in the subject and, yes, we could bring the project to his congregation.

In October 1999, we began the project with the first of what we hope will be ten to twelve Jewish congregations in the greater Chicago area. While we have only completed the project in four Jewish congregations as of this date, this anecdote might be interesting to note. As we presented the project at the first temple we visited, our experience felt like every other church basement we had been in before, filled with people who had had experiences of the presence or action of God in their lives and were happy to share their words and stories with us. Once again, for many it was the first time they had shared their story with anyone.

We were profoundly grateful to find the same gracious welcoming in the Jewish community that we found in the Christian community. It felt like another miraculous gift to treasure and cherish. We were also given Hebrew text to bring into our Jewish experience that provided us with words of God's loving actions within the Jewish community—words that would enrich our lives as well:

From the daily prayerbook:

> *How splendid is your light*
> *Which worlds do reflect!*
> *My soul is worn from craving*
> *For your love's delight.*
> *Please, good God, do heal her*
> *And show to her your face,*
> *So my soul can see you*
> *And bathe in your grace.*
> *There she will find strength*
> *And healing in this sight.*
> *Her joy will be complete then,*
> *Eternal her delight.*

From the weekday evening service:

Compassionate source of healing,
Heal us and we shall be healed;
Save us and we shall be saved;
Grant us a perfect healing for all our infirmities.

The final text has been a part of our project, used with all our groups, from the very beginning. These beautiful words from the Hebrew Scripture have been read at every meeting we have held: From Psalm 30:

Oh, Lord my God,
I cried to you for help
And you have healed me.

When people get together to share their experiences of the action or presence of God in their lives, the differences between us are subsumed in the similarities of our experiences. The project had opened us to a new appreciation of the working of the Spirit in the lives of all people; a discovered unity that was breathtaking; a new way of dialogue and connection, and another gift!

In the next section of this book, you will read some of the words and stories that others have shared about their own experiences of spiritual healing from Protestants, Catholics, and Jews. (We think you might find it difficult to identify which stories are which!) As you read these words and stories, let them speak to your heart. Each one of them carries a message of hope and healing and perhaps one of them will touch your life. Their gift to us . . . is our gift to you.

In the final section of our book, we will share with you what we have learned from our quest to find the meaning of the words "spiritual healing." We will also suggest some ideas about how you might open your life to God's healing presence. This will not be a "how-to" list of steps to be taken or strategies to be tried. It doesn't work that way. But it will reflect the ways in which our lives were utterly changed by the gift of the project. We offer our story as a direct invitation for you to engage in your own journey with God.

We have discovered that to travel with God is to follow an amazing path that is unpredictable, awesome, marvelous, scary, astonishing, breathtaking, life-changing, gut-wrenching, wondrous, mysterious, totally out of your control, confusing, unsettling, anxiety provoking, wonderful, and indescribable. It is the path that opens the door to God. Take it, and expect that life will turn upside down and change before your very eyes. Don't take it, and God will find another opportunity to knock on your door.

But know that God's promise to be with each of us will persist no matter what we do, and our healing will begin whenever we say that wondrous and life-giving word: "Yes!"

PART II
WORDS, LESSONS AND STORIES

CHAPTER 5. FIRST CAME THE WORDS

We were in the car on such a tight schedule that both of us were crabby under the pressure of having to get somewhere fast. That meant, of course, that we weren't speaking very much to each other. My husband was concentrating on driving, and I was spending my time trying not to worry about how late we were going to be.

For no particular reason that I can remember, we started to talk about the strangest thing. We got to talking about fairy tales and kingdoms, and I suddenly wondered why there were no "queendoms." I mean, why just kingdoms? The tension between us immediately eased and we started to imagine what a "kingqueendom" or a "queenkingdom" might be like. The words triggered an entire picture of a place where all are loved and peace prevails, a kind of modern-day Garden of Eden right there with us.

Suddenly, the car was filled with the loving and healing presence of God, and we were back in the place we belonged. We still use the words when we need to find a place of peace.

✣ ✣ ✣

IN EACH CHURCH we visited, we first asked for the words that people associated with the words "spiritual healing." We simply raised the questions of meaning and definition. When you hear the words "spiritual healing," what do you think of? If someone asked you what spiritual healing was, what would you tell them? If pressed to answer the question, "What is spiritual healing for you?" what would you say?

We explained that we were trying to build a vocabulary that people could use to talk about spiritual healing. If people find the subject matter difficult to describe or confusing to talk about, then we would be able to offer words that could be put together to form a definition and provide a language of healing. It was a good place to begin.

We also understood that words are the basic building blocks for stories and that if we could stimulate the sharing of words, we would also facilitate the offering of stories. In fact, the progression from words to stories was as natural as every other part of the project had been. People responded as if they could hardly wait for their words to be heard and recorded. In their thoughtful and serious considerations of the words of healing, we heard the prologue to the stories which would follow.

In sharing these words, simplicity seemed to offer the best structure available to us. The words presented themselves in a natural alphabetical order which allowed an almost poetic reading to take place. Each section of the alphabet includes both individual words as well as word phrases which people were eager to share and which we found particularly delightful.

As we have read and re-read these words, they seem to provide a marvelously simple way to reach into an interior spiritual place, forming a kind of prayerful mantra about spiritual healing. They present a peaceful entry into a space of reflection, and an invitation to linger a while, savoring each word and phrase, feeling and touching the simplicity and symmetry of this language of healing.

There is nothing complicated about these words, yet each carries a message of meaning and mystery; love and connection; truth and timelessness. They are a glorious compilation of over 2,500 voices raised in praise and gratitude. As you read them with loving care, may they speak to you of the Loving Care of the One who brought them to us.

We are privileged to be able to present them to you.

Spiritual healing is:

> Acceptance, awe, affirmation, answers,
> Assurance, abundance, awareness, aligned,
> Anticipation, atonement, at-one-ment, authentic,
> Alleluia!
> Accepting what you hadn't planned; accepting what you
>   didn't want to happen;
> (being) Awake!

Spiritual healing is:

> Belief, blessing, balance, beauty,
> Breath, bonding, birthing, buoyancy,
> Beginning, being different,
> Bliss!
> Being called by name; Being held in God's arms;
> Being put where you need to be; Being at home in the
>   moment;
> Becoming an insider;
> Being on cruise control with God keeping the speed!

Spiritual healing is:

> Comfort, connectedness, community, cleansing, creativity,

Courage, completeness, clarity, compassion, caring, contentment,

Christ, conversion, centered, calm, change,

Christian Science, charismatic, clearing out, cost,

Confession, commitment, confidence, closure,

Coming home!

Change of state: you feel better;

Continually being thrown on a potter's wheel with parts being stripped away and changing;

Cultivating an attitude of gratitude!

Spiritual healing is:

Discipline, discovery, deliverance, devotion,

Delicious!

Distinct, yet universal;

Direction out of the wilderness;

Despair is the movement of the soul toward healing;

(like) Dolphins following in God's wake!

Spiritual healing is:

Energy, empowerment, encircled, encompassing, endurance,

Excitement, elation, empathy, evangelism, ecstacy, eternal,

Enlightenment, ego-less,

Exhilaration!

Encircled in God's Love;

Everything in life is Spiritual Healing;

(an) Elusive moment of exquisite beauty!

Spiritual healing is:

Faith, forgiveness, freedom,

Filled, fulfillment, fearless, finding, flexibility,

Flame!

Fixing something that is broken;

Feeling grounded in the world, yet liberated from it;
Finding the Holy in the ordinary!

Spiritual healing is:
Grace, gratitude, growth,
Giving, guidance, generative, Gift!
Giving up the outcome;
God's ministry to us.

Spiritual healing is:
Hope, healing, Holy Spirit,
Humility, harmony, honesty, heaven,
Helping, happiness,
Holy!
Healing the patient doesn't mean curing the disease;
Healing is done by God, not us.

Spiritual healing is:
Integration, inspiration, immediacy,
Indebtedness, invoking,
Insight!
Intense awareness of being loved by God;
Insanity is doing the same thing, in the same way,
and expecting different results. Spiritual healing
breaks the cycle!
Immunization from past mistakes.

Spiritual healing is:
Joy, Journey,
Jesus!
(a) Journey to the very core of ourselves where God resides;
Just like love: you have to give it away to receive it!

Spiritual healing is:
> Knowledge,
> Kneeling!
> (the) Knowledge that healing takes place *is* the great gift!

Spiritual healing is:
> Love, letting go, learning,
> Listening, laughter, lightness,
> Liberation!
> Like a caterpillar, we end up wrapped in our own
>> little cocoon. Then we break out as a butterfly.
> (a) Lifelong dance of learning and practicing.

Spiritual healing is:
> Mystery, miracle, meditation, mindfulness,
> Mercy, mission, meaning, movement,
> Maturing, melting, mending, mind/body connection,
> Music!
> More of thee and less of me;
> (a) Moment of awareness when I say "Yes!"
> (the) Mystery of the Mystery!

Spiritual healing is:
> Newness, new life, new beginning, new directions,
> Nurture!
> (the) Natural state of our relationship with God;
> Never complete—always in process.

Spiritual healing is:
> Openness, obedience, oneness, opportunity,
> Out of control,
> Ordinary, ongoing, optimistic, overcoming,
> Outrageous Joy!

(being) Open to the irrational and the unexpected
    opportunity.
Once received, you have a responsibility to do something:
    to take action!

Spiritual healing is:
    Peace, prayer, process,
    Powerful, patience, possibility, paradox,
    Positive thinking, purpose, presence, perspective,
        persistence,
    Pain, progress, pristine, purging,
    Promise!
    Partnership with God;
    (a) Paradigm shift;
    (the) Possible of God in the midst of our impossible;
    Profound Love!

Spiritual healing is:
    Quiet!
    (Learning to be) Quiet and listen.

Spiritual healing is:
    Reconciliation, release, relief, renewal,
    Resurrection, recovery, reunion, reassurance, redemption,
    Risk, return, reverence, respect,
    Repent, revealed, relinquish, relationship,
    Restless, remembering, receive, resolution,
    Rediscovery, reawakening, remission, recycling,
    Recreation, resurrendering, rededication, retrospective,
    Reborn!
    Respect God's timing: God is never late!
    (the) Restoring of the soul;

Reawakening of the known but forgotten;
Radical dependency!

Spiritual healing is:

Surrender, surprise, submission, serenity, strength,
Sharing, seeking, service, support,
Salvation, sureness, silence, solitude,
Synchronicity, searching, simplify, safety,
Security, sincerity, struggle, shift,
Soul, soul mending, soul-va-tion;
Sunshine!
Spiritual healing is a life preserver;
Spiritual healing breaks the crust;
Spiritual healing is a second chance!

Spiritual healing is:

Trust, transformation, touch, thanksgiving,
Tears, truth, transcendent, time,
Transfigured, trans-rational, transmutation, together,
Topsy Turvy!
There is a divine structure in the ugly moments of life that
    needs to be discovered;
The surround of God's love.

Spiritual healing is:

Understanding, unplanned, unexpected, unconditional,
Uplifting, unlimited, unearned,
Unafraid, unselfish, unlearning,
Unity!
(being) Used by God;
Unexpected joy!

Rev. Bobbie McKay, Ph.D., and Lewis A. Musil, M.A.

Spiritual healing is:
>   Victory, vitality, vulnerable,
>   Vortex!
>   (God's) Vision of who we are as opposed to who we think
>   we are;
>   (a) Verb;
>   Victory over victimization!

Spiritual healing is:
>   Wholeness, work (hard work!),
>   Warmth, wisdom, waiting, willingness,
>   Wonder, wonderful,
>   Witnessing, wounded, weaving together, weeping,
>   Wow!
>   (a) Wake up call;
>   (I am) Willing, please make me able;
>   What other kind of healing is there?

Spiritual healing is:
>   Yes, yoke,
>   Yahoo!
>   (if) You pray for something specific, and don't get an answer,
>   That *is* the answer.

The one word that seemed to describe spiritual healing for most people was the word "peace." That "peace" was more specifically described as "the peace that passes all understanding," the "peace" that transcends happiness or joy, the "peace" that one feels at the core of one's being, the "peace" that is recognizable and is experienced as a change of state which could last for a brief moment or for an indeterminate period of time.

Each word listed as the first word in the alphabetical presentation was the word that we heard most often in that category. In

summarizing our words, therefore, we could look at the definition of spiritual healing as a loving lyric in a universal song
written by a compassionate creator who invites each one of us to
enter into the mystery of connection.

Spiritual healing is:
Acceptance,
Belief,
Comfort,
Discipline,
Energy,
Faith,
Grace,
Hope,
Integration,
Joy,
Knowledge,
Love,
Mystery,
Newness,
Openness,
Peace,
Quiet,
Reconciliation,
Surrender,
Trust,
Understanding,
Victory,
Wholeness,
Yes!

These words speak for themselves, in the language of spiritual healing.

CHAPTER 6. LESSONS AND PREPARATIONS

It was one of those days when nothing goes right. We got up late, had to be on the road fast, hadn't slept enough hours, and were needing to get a fast breakfast. Of course, when you want something to work, it never does.

The restaurant was empty when we arrived, but then there wasn't a waitress around either. People started to come in, the waitress appeared but she waited on everyone else first. We were annoyed and frustrated. Breakfast was cold ... so what else was new. We left in disgust, half running down the long corridor to the parking lot, feeling put-upon and angry.

As we started to pull out of our parking place, someone pounded on the door of our van. I looked out and saw the waitress from the restaurant holding my purse. She had to have literally run the distance from the restaurant to our car in order to catch us. She was breathless, but more than that, she had a look on her face of such concern and care that I couldn't speak for a moment. I finally stumbled around the words of thanks and recovered enough to look for some money to tip her for her effort.

She looked shocked. "I don't want a tip. I just wanted you to have your purse." I thanked her and then watched her walk away, back to her job. I was stunned. The gift she had given me was far greater than my purse. This was God

*present, God caring, God concerned, wanting me to have
what I needed. It was that simple. God was right there. All I
had to do was open my eyes and my heart to recognize it.*

IN MOST of our churches, we played a question "game" that
most people understood was facetious. It was intended to be a
further step in our journey of discovery and definition, another
way to explore spiritual healing. In effect, we played a game of
"What if." What if someone came to you and said, "I've heard
about this wonderful thing called spiritual healing. How do I get
it?" How would you respond? What would you say?

Almost immediately, someone would say, "Well, you don't
get it! It's a gift" and we would all agree that it was a foolish
question. Spiritual healing is not a commodity to be purchased
or acquired. That's not how it works. But if pressed further, and
especially in the light of the urgent need for spiritual healing in
the world today, people became seriously involved in a
thoughtful inquiry about a question that needed to be answered,
and which had no simple answer and no instant solution.

At no time did anyone feel they could provide the answer to
this question which has no answer; nor could they provide a
series of steps guaranteed to solve the problem. But people did
present us with a marvelous "Directory of Lessons and
Preparations" that one might consider as a possible pathway
toward the subject of spiritual healing. These were direct and
loving expressions of their own personal struggles to grapple
with the questions we would all like to have answered. *How do I
get it? Where can I go for help? I need some relief from my pain and I
don't know what to do. Give me a program or a plan.*

We present their responses as another loving gift to center

our hearts on the subject of spiritual healing and the Creator God who so generously surprises us with all the answers we need.

LESSONS:

ON GOD:

1. Talk to God; ask God for what you need; fall in love with God;
2. Take God seriously; trust that God is there;
3. Let God in; spend time with God; be hungry to know God;
4. Be honest with yourself in God's presence and be obedient to God's will;
5. Know that God is the answer; God has the answer;
6. Let go and let God; surrender your agenda for God's agenda;
7. To keep God in your mind, keep love in your heart.

ON JESUS:

1. Seek Jesus;
2. Love Jesus;
3. Repent, ask for forgiveness, and take Jesus into your heart;
4. Knowing Jesus means knowing ourselves.

ON PRAYER:

1. Prayer is a shortcut to God;
2. Pray without ceasing;
3. "Thy will be done" is a doorway to healing;
4. Sometimes you have to hit bottom before you learn to pray;
5. Start with prayer—end with prayer.

ON CHURCH AND COMMUNITY:

1. Go to church; read the Bible; read the psalms; take communion;
2. Find a pastor who believes in spiritual healing;

3. Find a community;

4. If you can't find a community, create one.

ON SHARING, WITNESSING, AND TESTIMONY:

1. Start with prayer and testimony;

2. Tell your story;

3. Listen to the experiences of others; it's how we connect;

4. Sharing and caring heals us;

5. Sharing teaches us we are all one in the spirit;

6. Surround yourself with people who are spiritually minded.

ON PAIN (SPIRITUAL, PHYSICAL, EMOTIONAL):

1. Know that God will always be found in the pain and struggle;

2. Stop running away from your pain—face it;

3. Pain is a beginning, not something to be removed;

4. Healing is on the other side of pain;

5. Sometimes you have to become empty in order to be filled;

6. Let yourself go and be weak;

7. Learn you can't handle it alone;

8. We all need to be "detoxed" because we're all in "recovery."

ON GIFTS AND GIVENS:

1. Spiritual healing is a gift and a blessing;

2. You have to allow it to happen and experience it;

3. It's a gift. There are no formulae to follow. There is no right or wrong way. There are many paths and every path is different.

4. It's a gift: something I have to work *at,* not *for;*

5. It's a lifelong learning process;

6. It's a lifelong journey: be patient;
7. It's always a mystery, a surprise, out of my control;
8. It's a given, just like God, like grace, and it happens all the time;
9. Spiritual healing always exceeds our expectations; it makes unexpected sense;
10. We need to receive the gift, not get it.
11. The first step is always: What do I have to give up? What do I have to do?
12. You're already there if you're asking the questions!

PREPARATIONS:

A. Realize that you have a problem:
1. Trust that God is with you;
2. Believe that spiritual healing happens;
3. Name it; know it exists; wake up to it; recognize it happens all the time;
4. Stop, look, listen;
5. Be willing to do the work;
6. Consciously choose God and a spiritual life;
7. Trust God with your heart, not your understanding;
8. Open your heart, get out of your head; you get it at the gut level;
9. Turn off your mind: logic will get in your way.
10. Be patient.

B. Give love and serve others:
1. Forgive others and ourselves;
2. Make amends and be responsible for your life;
3. Find a spiritual friend.

C. *Meet yourself and be accountable:*

1. Let go of the past;
2. Address your anger;
3. Get rid of self-pity; let go of your victim stance;
4. Live in the moment;
5. Do a lot of work on yourself;
6. Stop being ashamed of being religious;
7. Try solitude, silence, fasting, meditation.

D. *Release control:*

1. Surrender your self, your ego, your expectations, your plans;
2. Accept your limitations;
3. Be willing to let go of parts of yourself;
4. Stop trying to do too much;
5. Laugh;
6. Ask questions;
7. Try to be open;
8. Wait for the unexpected;
9. Get out of the way—let it happen;
10. Get out of the driver's seat and let go of your control; God's in charge.
11. Learn the difference between surrender and giving up.

E. *Share your story:*

1. Listen;
2. Be observant;
3. Be quiet;
4. Find a safe place to talk, a place where you feel special;
5. Study, go to classes, workshops; it's a learning process.

F. Challenge yourself:

1. Risk change and new behaviors;
2. Be willing to change;
3. Take action;
4. Persist and be tenacious;
5. Pull away from whatever is crowding you;
6. Push out the noise of the world;
7. Be open to possibilities;
8. Choose faith over fear;
9. Pray, focus on God, practice;
10. Just do it!
11. Practice God-talk.
12. Don't limit God.

G. A final lesson was presented as the generic summation of the whole process:

If you've got a problem and need spiritual healing:

—Don't nurse it;

—Don't curse it;

—Don't rehearse it;

Turn it over to God—

And God will reverse it!

CHAPTER 7. INTRODUCTION TO THE STORIES

When I was a freshman in college, I went to visit a friend who was very important to me. I don't remember what happened in that visit ... it was almost fifty years ago. But I remember being very unhappy and afraid I had said or done the wrong thing. Whatever it was, I went for a walk alone, desperately unhappy and feeling like the end of the world would be better than what I was experiencing.

Suddenly, the fear and the pain lifted. It was like the sun had come out from a deep and dark storm, radiating light and peace everywhere. I had no idea how or why it happened. But I felt a spiritual connection so deep that it filled my entire body. The anguish was totally gone. It was my first glimpse of the Peace of God ... the peace that passes all understanding. It changed everything.

ALL OF US are storytellers. Storytelling is such an ingrained habit that we are unaware that most of our interactions with people are the telling of stories to each other about who we are and what has happened to us. It is clear why. Unless the other person actually shares the event, the only thing that you can tell another about your experience is a story about it. You cannot tell events, only stories.

Jesus was a great storyteller, frequently confounding and opening up the understanding of his audience with parables, a form of the short, short story. Most of our knowledge of him comes primarily from four great storytellers: Matthew, Mark, Luke, and John. He represents the hero of the great story, the story of God in the world. His stories were based on the ancient heritage of the Jewish Law and Tradition.

In our travels to churches and temples around the country, we expected and hoped to find stories from people about spiritual healing, and find them we did. From beautiful sanctuaries to cramped church basements, people poured out their stories of the action of God in their lives. These stories represented overwhelming and life-changing experiences for each of them. Each story was a healing story, and a transformation of infinite value.

We did not know in advance what kind of stories they would be, but they do seem to arrange themselves in a particular way. In no special order, we heard stories of surprise at the actions of God; stories of physical curing; stories of disease where there was no evidence of physical curing, but where healing occurred; stories where there was no disease but a profound sense of healing was experienced. We heard conversion stories; stories of the presence of God. We were touched by "why me" stories, not as a negative expression of frustration and anger, but rather the "why" of amazement and awe for the mystery and wonder of God's presence and grace.

We found that in one sense, there was only one story, repeated in hundreds of different settings. Each story is a story of the perceived action or presence of God in people's lives. Sometimes, God acts directly in our lives and the results are always life-changing!

We have organized the stories in three categories:

1. Stories of spiritual healing when there is no disease present;
2. Stories of spiritual healing where there is a disease and a physical cure, often called a miracle cure, as a part of the healing;
3. Stories of spiritual healing in which there is a disease, with no physical cure, but in which there has been a profound sense of spiritual healing.

We were deeply touched by these stories and found that we were as much changed by the experience of listening to them as they had been life-changing for those who were sharing them. Each story carried the power of conviction and faith without the attempt to convince or preach. The honesty of the experiences they shared were like moments of truth which had transformed their lives. The depth of feeling expressed, often accompanied by tears, painted a picture of an experience that would never be forgotten and which was as powerful in the retelling as it had been in the original event, no matter how long ago it had happened.

It is very hard to translate the impact of the stories and give you a real-life picture of our experience in hearing them. In effect, we can only tell you another story from our experience of hearing literally hundreds of stories about the presence and action of God in people's lives. Words cannot quite capture the flesh and blood quality of what it meant to actually be there and hear stories that had never been told before; stories that had been told many times, but which still were accompanied by tears and deep feelings; stories that were remembered in some inner place, but which came to life in our setting of encouragement and care.

While we would have liked to share all the stories we heard (well over eight hundred), we selected the following stories as representative of the marvelous diversity in our sample. We have organized the stories as previously stated. But within each category the stories are presented in a random selection as they were presented to us.

We invite you to try to bring these stories to life as you read them, to imagine yourself in the experience and to sense the wonder, awe, and amazement that each person tried to convey in the telling of their stories. For each person, the event described became their transformation, their awareness of the presence of God in their life. They knew they were changed by the experience. They knew that something had happened to them which they described as an identifiable change of state. In time, they knew that the change they had experienced was permanent and indelible.

We can only express our deepest gratitude that the participants in the Spiritual Healing Project were willing to share their lives and stories so generously in order that we might bring them to you. We hope that these stories will ignite your own spiritual stories and bring you into deeper connection with God who has created all our stories and with the community of faithful who must tell and retell them as their Gospel of faith and truth.

If these transforming events can happen to so many people, from so many different backgrounds and walks of life, then they can happen for you. Perhaps they already have, and these stories can help you identify them as the presence of God in your life.

CHAPTER 8. STORIES OF SPIRITUAL HEALING

WHEN my son was in his mid-twenties, he contracted leukemia. I was devastated but determined to pray to God to heal him. Not only was I praying for his cure almost constantly, but I organized several churches in town to pray for him as well as churches in other parts of the country. I was determined that he would get well. Instead, he got worse and worse!

One day, I decided it was time to have it out with God and set God straight about this. I prayed for a long time and finally said, "God, you don't know what it's like to be a mother and have a son who is dying!" Then I stopped and realized what I had just said. I said to God, "Well, I guess you do know what it's like to have a son who is dying because you had one and he did die. What's more, you could have saved him. . . . But you didn't."

And then I said the hardest words I have ever spoken. "Okay. All right. I give it up. If he lives, you know that's what I want, and if he dies, that's . . . that's all right too. I put it in your hands."

And in that moment, I was healed. All the control and the push and the struggle and the demands were gone and I felt a deep sense of peace. Six months later, my son remitted . . . but that is another story. This was my story and my healing.

THERE are three things you have to relax and let go of if you want to do them properly: swimming, acting, and . . . surrendering to God. I know. It happened to me. I was trained to be a lawyer . . . had a good education. You need to be arrogant to be a lawyer and I was very good at that. When I was a graduate teaching assistant, I had a professor who gave me a lot of grief. I was not happy about that—and not very happy about other things in my life either. So I started to read Paul Tillich as a way of trying to make sense of things, to get some kind of perspective on life.

I was also doing a lot of acting at various places. But it just seemed to come to me that what I really wanted to be was a singer. I decided I'd better get some vocal training so I asked around and someone at church recommended the choir director. The choir director asked me to join the choir. I was concerned about this. I didn't know if I would feel accepted or not . . . I was afraid I'd be ignored. But I was pleasantly surprised. They were quite welcoming.

But still, my life got worse . . . a lot worse. Finally, I went to the associate pastor who really pastored me. We talked theology, not counseling. He said I was walking around the whole problem of faith and that I was having a spiritual struggle. I thought he might be right . . . but it didn't quite connect to where I was.

In 1974, the Sunday before worldwide Communion Sunday, I was singing a service for the handicapped. A friend was preaching the sermon and I heard him say:

"If you can bring yourself to confess and surrender to God, God will come to you." These were words I noted, but they didn't make any difference to me. Instead, I seemed to get more and more desperate. By the following Sunday, I was near suicide. I couldn't understand what was happening to me. None of it made any sense.

I was at the church service, and finally all I could do was to close my eyes and say, "I give up! I can't live like this. Whatever you want is okay with me."

Like that! Something passed through my whole body. I was stunned, but I knew I was changed. I went to see my pastor friend to tell him what happened. He looked at me and said, "You've had a conversion experience."

I knew he was right. I can't explain what happened. It was overwhelming. My life is completely changed. All the despair and hopelessness is gone.

I learned that God may not be in a hurry, but God is never late.

✤ ✤ ✤

THIS STORY took place in a church in the heroin district of Baltimore. It is estimated that in the sixteen blocks surrounding this church there are 17,000 heroin addicts.

IT'S BEEN five years now . . . on November 7th . . . that I've been clean from drugs and alcohol. I grew up with a lot of fear and low, low self esteem. When I found drugs and booze it seemed the answer I was looking for. It really seemed to help. But after a while, I saw that I still had the same problems . . . but now I was addicted, too. Things got worse and worse. I struggled but couldn't stop.

It was some of the people here, in this church—I didn't even know them—that helped me to stop . . . to get into treatment. We talked here in this room and I went to an N.A. meeting. When the meeting was over, they asked me what I was going to do now. I said to them, "Go home." But the church people wouldn't hear of that. Instead, several of them took me to Mercy Hospital. We sat there and talked from 9:30 A.M. to 6:00 P.M. I believe God was present there. These people had no experience with drugs. I think God told them what to do. Finally, I went into treatment. I wanted to quit, but I was scared. I prayed the first night that God would help me do it. I knew I couldn't on my own.

I began to get better. When the twenty-eight days of treatment were over, I got terrific support from this church. I was really surprised how much they cared. I was still scared, but I was so moved by their caring. It took five years for me to get where I am now. But now I'm outspoken and I fight for what I believe in. But mostly, I'm strong spiritually through prayer and through my healing.

It's not just that I don't need drugs. I know now that I'm worth something. I pray to God to use me and I choose faith over fear. I've gone from being a heroin addict to a church elder. Talk about a changed life! I've had many spiritual gifts. When I say I choose faith over fear I mean that waking up and knowing that I don't have to hunt around for drugs . . . that's a good day . . . it's having a second chance.

IN 1991, seven of us went up into the boundary waters at the U.S. and Canadian borders to do some fishing. During a sudden and very violent storm, we made for the nearest island and were just able to make it. But that wasn't the end of it. We were all, every one of us, struck by lightning. After it happened, I was on the ground . . . and not able to move. I lay on my back and looked up into the sky. . . . It seemed to open up and I had the feeling that I was looking into another world . . . maybe heaven . . . and I knew that God was there. I realized that God wasn't finished with me yet . . . then there was this light all around me . . . I can't explain any of it.

But then I looked at one of the others who was lying next to me and saw that he was having seizures. I was able to get up and go to him. I held him and helped him to wake up. The experience makes me feel very humble. We all survived. . . . Even though it was seven years ago, we still get together to talk about it. . . . We could never forget it. It was a very powerful, bonding experience.

MY SPIRITUAL healing began with a question asked forty years ago. I had been an active church member as a young person and was drafted during World War II. I had a furlough and some of my buddies and I went into the city. When we got off the train, some people I didn't know asked if we would like a free dinner. Now, people used to kid me that I would go anywhere for a free meal . . . probably true . . . and this time was no exception.

They took me to their church for dinner and afterward, we paired off to talk. My partner and I went to the altar and he asked me if I was a Christian. I always thought I was. But that day, when I said it out loud, somehow it made a real difference. That was the day I made my commitment, my first real commitment to being a Christian. Things can happen in such strange places.

Christianity is like love: you have to give it away to receive it. Whenever I think of this, my tears always flow . . . just like now. I can't explain it. But I was changed just saying the words out loud.

LAST MARCH, my son contracted a difficult illness. . . . It seemed to make him more and more withdrawn and finally, he was unable to leave the house. I was really unhappy. Everything we tried was no help. We tried various doctors, different therapies, and the whole thing only got worse. I didn't know what to do, but I was really frustrated for him and for all of us.

Last summer I went on a retreat. I had to get away. The harder I worked on getting a handle on his problem, the worse it got. Well, anyway, I was at this retreat and there was this dog there that I liked to play "stick" with. He recognized me and we started to play. I would throw the stick and he would fetch it. But then, after a few times of throwing and bringing back, the dog wouldn't release the stick. He just wouldn't let go. I was pulling, he was tugging . . . and I was getting more and more frustrated. Finally, I almost screamed at the dog, "Scamper, if you would just let go, you would have a lot more fun."

When I said that it was like being hit by a lightning bolt. I realized that I was the one who had to let go. I had to let go of trying to fix my son's situation. I wasn't able to "play" at anything when all I could think about was how to make my son better. I had to let go and see what would happen. It absolutely changed my life. My son still has his problems, but I'm no longer obsessed with making him better.

MY DAUGHTER and I have not had the easiest of relationships. Somehow, we always ended up in some kind of squabble or fight. Nothing ever seemed to work between us. You know how that happens sometimes.

Well, when she was in college, over the summer she worked at a camp for disadvantaged children in the East. Before she left home, we had had a fight over her determination to marry a man who was quite unsuitable for her, at least in my opinion. I stewed about this for a while, and then I called her up and asked if I could come out to visit her. She said she had one day off and if I could make it on that day to come ahead.

As I got on the plane to fly out, there were a number of professional football players also getting on the plane. I thought to myself, I hope one of them does not decide to sit next to me. I wanted to be left alone to think about what I wanted to say to my daughter and to figure out how to get her to change her mind about this guy. I was really determined to straighten her out and I needed some time to get prepared.

Well, none of the football players sat next to me. But instead a tall Native American man sat down, and I reluctantly fell into conversation with him. We talked about spiritual books, and finally he asked me where I was going. I told him that I was going East to see my daughter. And then he asked me what my daughter was doing. With some slight irritation in my voice, because I really didn't want to be talking to him about her, I said something about the fact that she worked at a camp for disadvantaged children. I wished he would leave me alone.

But then he said something that really caught me off guard . . . he said, "Your daughter is a healer." I was astonished by his words. I had never thought of her this way before. His statement seeemed to open up my whole being . . . my entire orientation toward my daughter changed in that instant. It was such an incredible experience that I wouldn't have been at all surprised if he simply dematerialized when we got to the airport instead of walking off the plane.

I saw my daughter and said nothing of what I had gone there to say. We had a wonderful time . . . we still are. Our relationship is absolutely changed!

I JUST HAVE to say that something is happening here, in this group tonight, that is very healing. I really appreciate being here tonight. I wasn't planning on coming here, but I did. I came in from about fifty miles away . . . and this experience has turned out to be terribly important to me. There is healing happening right here. I can feel it.

MOST of my life I have spent in some diet regimen or another. I have gained and lost over a ton in that time. Last year, I started to gain again and it began to affect me physically as well as emotionally. My sister-in-law got me the Cleveland diet, but that didn't work. Finally, I went to an "expert" who told me what to do. I gained six pounds on his diet. I was beside myself . . . desperate, and with no hope of ever changing the situation.

I stood on the scale, disgusted with myself, having eaten my way through the Super Bowl game, and started to cry. I said to God, "You'll have to help me, I can't do it." And I meant precisely that.

Since then, I've lost thirty-four pounds and it's staying off. That moment on the scale was a transforming moment.

I THINK of this story as the "event of the path." I grew up Catholic, but had long ceased to practice it. My wife and I were at a resort in Oklahoma . . . we were essentially nonreligious at that time. We thought of ourselves as "realists" and would make fun regularly of Oral Roberts and the faith healers on television.

I remember that the resort was named "Shangri-La." Well, on Saturday, as I was heading for the putting green, I passed a worship service going on in a room in the hall where I was walking. The door was open. I stopped, not intending to go in . . . and then something just drew me into the room. I sat down, stayed through the service, and then went back to our room. I didn't go to the putting green. Instead, I saw my wife and told her that something had "clicked."

The next day, I found out that my grandmother had died at the exact moment that I went into that worship service. This impressed both of us . . . and we made some jokes about connections, I guess to cover our feelings. But it turned out to be a healing experience.

We started to go to church regularly, and although we didn't talk a lot about it, our state is really changed. We didn't feel we had to analyze it . . . but just to go with it. And we have. And we are changed.

MY SPIRITUAL healing happened this summer. I was a brand-new hospital chaplain and the first time I saw someone die was very upsetting. I was frightened and confused by my feelings. I didn't know quite what to do. I found myself saying to God, "Where are you?"

Later I saw a second person die . . . but this was very different. This death was peaceful, and I realized that death was a natural process, the completion of life. I waited until the medical team left the patient, and then went back into the room and prayed a prayer of gratitude to God for this death and my enlightenment about death. It was a remarkable experience, and a healing for me.

MY FIRST brush with death as an ordained minister was when I was invited by a family to be present to their dying mother—a woman I had known before I was ordained. I was very nervous about visiting her . . . what would I say? What did I know about death? How could I be helpful when I was so nervous?

When I arrived, she was peaceful and ready to die. She had waited for her family to all get there and I watched as I saw them relate to her. . . . I'm sorry, I can't tell this story without tears. I realized that I was being healed. The love simply flowed from her and flowed back to her from her family. It was God's love that was flowing between all of us. She was being loved as she died.

I still have a total sense of that day which was an unbelievable experience for me and it transformed my ministry. The memory is as alive today as it was then. I will never forget it.

IN 1979, my brother was murdered. They caught the man who did it and brought him to trial. He was put in prison awaiting execution. I was very troubled . . . and could find no peace about what had happened. I needed to know why—why did this happen to my brother? Why would someone murder him? I finally had to come to Chicago which was where my brother was killed to find some answers. . . . I had to do something. I contacted a minister there and actually stayed with him, talking to him about my story and my pain.

Finally, with his help, I resolved to see the man, the man who killed my brother. I needed to confront him directly. The minister said I should do that, and I knew that he was right. I didn't have a choice.

I met the man face to face and asked him, "Why? Why did you do this?" He couldn't really answer my question. But he asked me for forgiveness. After that, I was able to go on with my life. This has somehow allowed me to be healed. My family is not healed. But I am.

I GREW UP in the church and when World War II came along, I joined up and was taken prisoner in Germany. During my internment, I found that the human spirit was capable of undying strength against cruel and inhumane punishment. Somehow my faith and prayers enabled me to be of help to others.

I met a man in the camp who was a Presbyterian minister. He felt he was not a particularly effective minister in his civilian life. But in the camp, he became transformed into a powerful, healing agent. The prison camp was his finest ministry. He found that through the spirit he grew to meet the needs of others. For him, it was a strange kind of healing that allowed him to minister as he had always wanted.

Rev. Bobbie McKay, Ph.D., and Lewis A. Musil, M.A.

I KNOW that touch may be healing. In 1990, my mother came to live with us. It soon became apparent that she had Alzheimer's disease. We put her in a day-care program, but she simply got worse and worse. I went to a support group and it helped me in some ways. But pretty soon, my mother became housebound. She couldn't go to the day care anymore. And I could feel the pressure really building in me. I felt like I was carrying everyone on my back, and it was breaking under the strain.

I had to dress and undress her. She was incontinent and so I had to clean her up. It was really tough. I spent a lot of time grieving over this . . . the support groups were some help. I learned some coping techniques and tricks to make things work better. But then it got really bad. I felt absolutely alone. It didn't matter, though. I still had to cope with the whole thing myself.

One day I was trying to get her dressed. I wanted her to brush her teeth so we could go to the doctor's office. She was impossible . . . waving the toothbrush around, smearing toothpaste on the mirror. I knew I was losing it. I couldn't help myself. I heard myself shouting at her, "You'll be the death of me!" I wanted to take that toothbrush and just jab it into her, stab her with it.

My mother was oblivious to me and my feelings. I was ready to snap. Then suddenly, I felt two huge hands on my back. I was sure it was God. No one was in the room, but suddenly I was not alone. No words were spoken but everything changed. The anger drained away, and I felt . . . peaceful. Mother was just the same, but I was different. Suddenly, I could cope. I hadn't asked for help. But the help came just when I needed it.

To this day, that event makes everything possible in my life. It even carries over into other parts of my life. Now I know I can talk with God, especially when things get hard. It was a healing for me even though I know that my mother will only get worse.

✤ ✤ ✤

I MET my husband when I was fifteen years old. It was love at first sight . . . for him, too. Five years later, we were married and everything was perfect. He was wonderful and we were very happy. We had a little boy, and our family felt complete. We had been married eleven years.

In 1973, he killed himself. He put a gun to his head and pulled the trigger. Later, I found out it was supposed to be a double killing. The police psychologist—he was a cop—told me so. My husband had talked to some of his friends about killing himself. He knew it would be terrible for me and so he said "he would take care of that too."

On the day he killed himself, I was working upstairs cleaning. He was down in the recreation room in the basement watching television. At least, I guessed he was watching something on television. Three times he called for me to come down to see him. The first time, I started to go down, but my son needed something and I was delayed. He called again and the second time . . . it had gotten dark now . . . my son called out again and I went to see him. The third time I started to go down stairs, but he said, "never mind" and I went on with my cleaning.

I heard a noise, but thought it was a truck backfiring. I was wrapping something and finished the job. Then I went downstairs to take the trash out. As I opened the door, the dog came running in, went down to the basement and made a terrible sound. I didn't pay much attention, but simply emptied the trash, got the vacuum cleaner and started downstairs.

As I passed the recreation room, I saw my husband sitting in his chair. I called to him, but he didn't answer. I was busy running the vacuum and didn't bother to stop. But when I finished, I came back and saw his head slumped onto his chest. It looked like he had thrown up. I went over to him to help him, and as I tried to turn his head, my hand went completely inside of it.

I was . . . I can't find a word to describe my feelings. I saw the gun and picked it up with the idea that I would kill myself. I felt dead anyway . . . in shock . . . whatever . . . I don't know. And then I thought of Jeremiah 27: "He has a plan for your life." So I put the gun down, turned from my dead husband and went up the stairs to my son. With each step, I felt life returning . . . and I knew that my spiritual healing had begun.

I was dead, and now I would live. This happened twenty-three years ago. I can still see it, but only in pieces. This is the first time I have tried to put it together . . . the first time I have ever told the whole story to anyone.

FIFTEEN years ago, our daughter died. There was a pretty good support group at the church and I came through it pretty well. But five years ago, our son died, too. It was awful . . . worse than awful . . . there aren't any words. Our children were gone. My husband had a new church now and there were no support groups around. What's more, the people didn't seem interested in talking about or dealing with my grief beyond just some surface stuff. They just didn't want to hear it. And so I shut down. I survived, but that's all. I was in terrible shape.

Some time later, I went on a retreat . . . I didn't look for anything to happen. I didn't expect any relief. I thought God had deserted me. But somehow, I came to realize that it was I who had deserted God. We were doing an art experience. I put on my headphones, listened to the music, and I started to draw. I found myself overcome with a sense of peace. I knew that everything would be okay, and that life would be different from then on.

It was, and it was a healing for me.

WHEN my husband died in his early fifties, I thought I handled it OK. . . . What can you do? But after a while, I wasn't feeling well physically. I got scared so I went to the doctor, who examined me and said, "There's nothing wrong with you . . . you're just grieving." He said something that sounded like I should go home and grieve. I didn't go home. I didn't feel good and I didn't want to be alone.

Instead, I stopped by a restaurant that we had visited a few times when my husband was alive. We went there for coffee . . . sometimes a meal. The waitress came over to me. I had seen her before at the restaurant, but didn't know her. I recognized her, but I was not feeling especially friendly.

She said to me, "You're not feeling well, are you?" I nodded, surprised that she had noticed. And then she said the most incredible thing. She said, "Would you like me to pray for you?" I was really taken aback, but thought for a moment and figured she meant she would include me in her prayers that night, or at church on Sunday, or something like that. So I said, "Yes." She must have known what I was thinking because she said to me, "No, I mean right here, now. I'd like to pray for you right now."

I hesitated, and then I nodded. I wasn't sure I could speak. She took my hands and there in the middle of that crowded restaurant, she prayed the most eloquent prayer I had ever heard. It was beautiful. I felt a marvelous calm. I felt healed.

Rev. Bobbie McKay, Ph.D., and Lewis A. Musil, M.A.

HEALING can be disconcerting and downright scary. I was a chaplain in a general hospital. A man in his sixties was admitted with an aneurysm. He was losing function and the family was called in. I was not involved with this part of it, but a day and a half later . . . after the family had assembled, I was asked to come in. He was in really bad shape, and was having great difficulty breathing.

The family asked me to pray for him. I said, "Okay. Tell me about him." They talked about him and then we held hands and prayed. I affirmed his love of life and thanked God for the past few hours when the family had gathered. I asked God for serenity for the family and asked God to hold him in the palm of his hand. Then he stopped breathing.

I thought to myself, "My God, I've killed him!" But then I realized that it was just that he had been healed enough to let go . . . indeed, that he had just experienced the ultimate healing: death. I knew that God was active in this process. I saw death in a new light. I finally learned to say, "Okay, God, whatever you're going to do is okay. I"ll try to be there to go along with it." It was a transformation for me . . . I was healed too.

THE JUDGMENT of others no longer affects me because of my relationship with God. It's really an authentic relationship. I was very grateful for my spiritual heritage being raised in a Midwest Quaker home. It was very important to me. But being a gay person I felt spiritually abused by the church . . . being a Christian seemed to be based on what you did not do, what you shouldn't do.

After a lot of hard times and painful experiences, I came to realize that that wasn't true. I said to my mother, "There is so much more to being a Christian than all the don'ts." This made me feel a little more healed. Maybe it was the beginning of my healing . . . my life seems to be always allowing God to heal me— sometimes physical, sometimes spiritual. But all the healings are so meaningful.

Ten years ago, a very dear friend was dying of AIDS. When I heard about it, I talked to the minister and he asked what the church could do for him. He had support from doctors, psychologists, and support groups. But he said, "I have no one to say my prayers with." That was the beginning of the HIV support group here.

There have been many healings over the years . . . not cures, but real healings. My friend was in a hospice unit so we took communion to him. When it came time to pass the peace, I took his hand and said, "Peace to you," and my friend was able to say to me, "Peace to you" . . . before he died.

Sorry, I can't help crying over the memory of that time because peace took on a whole new meaning for me then, as did communion. It was so important. I've never forgotten it.

✤ ✤ ✤

I WAS twenty-two and a full-blown agnostic. Science was my God. I was a biological sciences major and only believed in what I could prove and deal with. I threw out my entire Catholic baggage when I was eighteen. I resolved to live a good life and not set a bad example, but for the rest of it . . . that religious stuff . . . no way!

When I was in school, the electron microscope had just been invented. During one of my classes, I watched a film of the spermatogenesis of a grasshopper and watched myosis occur. I was knocked out! I said without even thinking about it, "There must be a God. There's no design without a designer!"

I openly wept and left feeling content . . . I was healed.

ONE TIME when I was barreling into church, late as usual, I saw a woman standing in the doorway waiting for a cab. I was feeling pretty down and depressed . . . and she seemed kind of anxious. I didn't know her—so I don't know why I did this . . . but I said to her, "Are you okay?" We started to talk, and I saw her perk up. I became animated too and soon I was smiling (and so was she) and God was present to both of us. She was changed . . . and so was I! It was that simple

I WAS DRIVING a friend home one night, when she told me of a very painful thing in her life. I listened, and then I stopped the car and took her hand. My friend said, "We can go on now." And I might have just done that. Ordinarily, I would have. But instead I said, "We should pray." I somehow knew that she wanted to pray too, but that's a hard thing to ask people to do.

Having said what I did, I didn't really know what to say. But I thought of the verse, "Be still and know that I am God." I don't know why . . . it just came into my head. But after that it was easy. That started it. God was there.

WE had been camping for about three weeks and I needed to go into town to get some things. My son wanted to go along and when we got there—it was a terribly hot day—he said that he didn't want to go to the store with me. And he didn't want to sit in the car and wait for me. What he wanted to do was to go down into the park by the river. I thought about it, and then said to him, "Okay, but be careful."

When I finished shopping and started back to my car, some boys came up and said that my son had gone into the river and was swept over the falls. I was frantic and very frightened. I wanted to pray but realized that God couldn't undo what was already done. I thought, maybe it was someone else . . . somebody else's son going over the falls. All the things that go through your head when you're desperate.

Then I had a sense of God's arms around me. I knew I would survive in God's love, even if the worst had happened . . . if my son had died. I said, "So that's what God's love is all about, that's what it means." And I felt so peaceful. It was amazing. When I got to the hospital, I found that my son was hurt, but not badly hurt, and that he would be okay. It was a transforming experience for me.

I LOST a sibling when I was a child and it affected me. Well, I didn't think it affected me very much . . . until I had a child of my own. When my daughter was born, I became obsessed with worry that she would die. I prayed about this, and one night, as I was kissing my daughter good-night, I realized that God loved her, too, and that God would take care of her.

I didn't realize this was a healing experience until just this very moment. Now I know.

A FIFTEEN-YEAR-OLD girl in our congregation was raped on the first day of school. The church called a meeting that night with everyone . . . the girl, her family . . . all the members of the church came and we openly expressed our tears and our love and support for the girl and her family. We organized an escort service for the girl . . . someone was always with her when she left home . . . even in going from class to class in school, after school too. She was protected everywhere she went until she felt safe again.

Finally, as a community we felt we had to do something about the person who raped her. He was known, and so we could talk to him. We brought him into the church too and he repented and asked her and her family for forgiveness. And they did forgive him. It was a miracle of healing for the entire church.

IN 1968, when I came to this country, I had to leave my family behind in the Philippines, including my daughter who was in high school. She got married about two years later, but she didn't tell me, nor did anyone else tell me right away. But other people knew about it. My brother finally told me and I hit the roof! The way I heard about it was that my brother called me and said, "Are you sitting down?" And then he told me. I cried all the time . . . every night. I just couldn't get over it. How could it happen without my knowing? Why would people keep it from me?

After a while, he calls me again and says, "How are you feeling?" And when I told him I was still really upset, he says, "Give it up!" But I didn't pay attention. It was not my plan that my daughter get married. But he kept calling, and finally I prayed to God. I said, "What will I do? I can't go back to the Philippines . . . shall I accept this? When I had left, my daughter was in school. She had a good future . . . what will it be now?"

One night, as I was praying, there was a sudden peace in my heart. I said, "I have been so nasty." I called my daughter and gave her my blessing, and for the first time I was able to sleep through the night. My heart was really changed. It was healed.

Now my daughter is here in this country with her children who are now twenty-five and twenty, and I love them all dearly.

I HAVE FOUND it very hard to forgive God for letting my best friend die at thirty-two. We all prayed for her . . . did all the right things . . . and she died. Until tonight, I have been very angry and unhappy. I couldn't understand why God would do this. It wasn't the way it was supposed to be.

But here tonight . . . I'm beginning to see that there was actually a great healing that happened to me through her dying. We became close, intimate in a way we would never have become if this had not happened. When we had all the time in the world, it was different. But when we knew this was happening . . . well, we just had a connection that meant everything to me. I miss her. . . . I don't like her being gone. But I'm seeing it differently here tonight . . . it really was a healing.

I HAVE two sons and they are both in jail. As if that wasn't bad enough, I got so involved with trying to get them the right lawyers to get out of jail, I was running around like a crazy person. It was so expensive! I had to work all the time to get enough money to pay the lawyers. This went on for three or four years.

Then one day, as I was visiting my youngest son, he said to me, "You're in the wrong struggle, Mom. You're a Christian . . . you don't need lawyers. Pray to God. You're trying to control all this. Give it up! I know I'm here for a purpose and I can trust God. I need to do my time . . . what I did was wrong."

Suddenly, I knew he was right. Now I can let it go . . . and I can open up to others . . . tell them my story. My sons will be free when the time is right. It's all changed for me. I can let it go and trust God. It really is a healing . . . for me.

IN MY THIRTIES, I was a mixed-up mom with four kids and a nice house . . . and I was miserable. I was searching for something and I didn't know what. I asked all kinds of questions about life. I thought of the disciples at Pentecost and I thought that there must be something in that story for me.

But I kept to myself and was just insecure about everything. Then one day, I just stopped and prayed, "Lord, if you really are real, I give you my life." Nothing happened right away. But later, while I was doing the dishes, I was surrounded by this great light. I knew it was God! It was all around me and . . . everything changed. Nothing changed on the outside, but everything was changed on the inside! I changed on the inside.

WE WERE foster parents and were given a child that was a real handful. We tried everything . . . and nothing worked. We were at our wits' end not knowing what to do, what to try. Finally, we reached the end of the road. We asked to have him removed. I felt like such a failure . . . so unworthy. It was hard to go to church. I felt so guilty and so undeserving.

One Sunday, I went early and sat in the sanctuary. It was communion Sunday, and I thought to myself, "I can't take communion because I don't deserve it." Then I heard a voice say, "No one deserves it . . . that's not why you're invited."

In that moment I discovered the grace of God. I was healed.

✣ ✣ ✣

WHEN my husband died eighteen years ago, he left me over $60,000 in debt. I shut down emotionally. I survived . . . but I did not mourn his death. I was too angry. I worked day and night to pay off the debt. I know what it is to go hungry.

Then I had to have major surgery. It was too much and I became quite bitter with everything. I had been bitter with the church because no one from the church came to visit me or help me after my husband's death. However, I knew there was something pushing me and that something drove me back to the church.

That was when I began my spiritual walk. For some reason, I was able to see that there were many blessings in my life which I had not seen before. I saw that it was not Jesus who had forsaken me, but I who had forsaken him. I finally opened up to Jesus and said, "Here I am, I give myself to you."

And my life has changed. My bitterness is completely gone. I sense that God has a plan for me and I am really open to it.

Rev. Bobbie McKay, Ph.D., and Lewis A. Musil, M.A.

I AM a doctor and a member of this church. One of our members became very ill and was hospitalized at the university clinic. I got involved with the family in order to comfort them. Maybe I did . . . I don't know.

But being with the family and feeling the sense of community between them and the patient has helped me to feel God in a way I had never felt before. I can see now that my soul was in a drought . . . and now the water is flowing. I can see the faith.

I WAS TRYING to manage my son's drug addiction. I was furious with God for letting him get on drugs. One day I called home from where I work to talk to his father, who said, "This is not the first time he's been on drugs." He started to give me a hard time, and I started to give him one back. We were both angry and frustrated with a situation that was out of control that we couldn't change.

Then I heard God say, "Sit down and shut up!" I did. And then God said, "Max needs his father." And I heard that too.

Later, I went on a retreat, and in the middle of it I was able to let go and realize that God was taking me to a place where God wanted me to go, the place I needed to be. I needed to let go . . . and that was my healing.

I WAS a pilot in the China-Burma-India theater during World War II. After the bomb at Hiroshima, we started to evacuate people in Okinawa so they could go home. I was flying my C47 on a clear night . . . it was a piece of cake. Everybody was on board . . . no trouble at all . . . and then, about halfway there, we were at ten thousand feet, both engines quit. I went through the procedures . . . full rich mixture of gas . . . pump up the gas . . . turn the engines on . . . then turn them off again . . . and on again . . . and still both engines didn't respond. They didn't do anything.

I told my copilot to get ready for a crash landing on the water. I prayed for the people on board and their families. I prayed for my family while we were descending.

At about three thousand feet, I turned on the landing lights so that I could see the waves and figure out how best to hit the water.

I ended my prayer and thought, "This is it" . . . and then suddenly, both engines cut in. I flew all the way to Shanghai and told them what had happened. They checked both engines and couldn't find anything wrong with either one. I know that prayer had a lot to do with it. I really know that.

SPIRITUAL HEALING is in everyday loving and caring. I was having an awful day . . . everything was going wrong. I felt terrible, worthless . . . didn't care about anything. Life wasn't worth very much at all.

Then my son put his arms around me and said, "But I love you, Mom."

I felt healed.

Rev. Bobbie McKay, Ph.D., and Lewis A. Musil, M.A.

THIS is a hard story to tell and I've never shared it with anyone. For a long time, I just didn't know whether to believe it happened or not . . . it was so strange, and yet I knew that it did happen.

Six years ago, I had lost touch with God and everything was a mess. I was raised Catholic but I had fallen away and as things got worse and worse, I got more and more desperate. Finally, I asked God to help me. I asked God every day to help me and nothing changed. I was furious. I felt like everything I had been told was a lie and that God didn't care.

Then one day, for some reason I don't quite understand, I began to think about all the things I had and I decided to go for a walk. As I was walking, someone grabbed my left hand. It felt good. I looked down, but there was no one there. But I knew that God had heard me and had reached out and held my hand to let me know that it would be okay. And it was.

I JUST got back from a centering prayer retreat. The last night we gathered in the meditation room. There were twenty-two of us at the retreat and we had to tell what the retreat meant to us. I really hated this part . . . it was uncomfortable for me.

But each person said such deep and wonderful things that by the time it came to me, I just started to talk and I realized while I was talking that I had had a healing! Later, after it was over, a woman came up to me and said, "I'm glad you had a healing." It felt good. God gives us so many surprising gifts. . . .

IN OUR company, there is a prayer team on the voice mail. It's extremely busy and we get a lot of feedback about how helpful it is.

Healing for me has been the times when I "weep for joy." At one of those times, a man said to me, "Jesus loves you . . . you know that, don't you?" I cried for twenty minutes and felt healed!

✜ ✜ ✜

THE LORD talks to us in so many ways. Sometimes God uses dreams to communicate. I took this trip to Montreal on the night train and fell asleep with my head against the window.

In my dream, I saw an article that I had read in the newspaper ten years ago. The article talked about how two trains had passed in the night, but that something was out of line and one train hit every other car of the other train. I awoke, and moved over to the other part of the compartment where I fell asleep again. Sometime later that night, our train car, while passing another train, was hit by that train in the exact spot where I was sitting. The whole side was torn up!

✜ ✜ ✜

JESUS says, "Your faith has healed you." Faith is committing to Jesus' healing plan. I was praying and taking an enormous amount of time explaining exactly what my intentions were and why I was praying this prayer.

Then, I interrupted myself, and I said, "For crying out loud, God knows if I'm sincere or not . . . so shut up!" I did, and I started a life of contemplative prayer. . . .

Over the years of being obedient to centering prayer, the rough edges have come off . . . the Lord is getting me un-junked. Believe me, that is a healing!

I CAN TRACE my spiritual healing to a folk mass at St. Lukes. I was at mass. I was raised to be a Catholic, but I was a heathen in the church. I went forward to get the blessing . . . but nothing happened. I felt empty.

Later, I went to see some friends who were having a spiritual healing group.

The evening was enlightening and I was energized by it. I told my mother about this and when I went upstairs I heard my mother say, "Thank you, Jesus." I said to her, "What are you thanking Jesus for?" And she said, "You needed something and you got it."

THERE'S a lot of living in dying. My father was dying and I nursed him until the day he died. It was sad, but once he had died, I realized what a profound experience we had had. If you want to know something about living, be with someone who is dying.

I grew immensely during his death. It was an amazing, really powerful, healing experience. It was the best relationship we'd ever had.

WE were talking about church rituals the other day. Our ritual of confession gives us a chance to see healing happen.

One day, as I was in the confessional box, a person came in and told me his story. It was a very troubling story. He would come in almost weekly and tell me the same thing, over and over again for a couple of years.

All of a sudden, he stopped coming. I felt very bad about this because I felt I had somehow let him down, or hadn't said the right thing or given him the help he needed. Then one day, I picked up the paper and read a story about a suicide. Although I didn't know this person's name or who he was, over time I had come to know him and some of the things in the article made me sure this was the person. I felt terrible. I was certain I had really failed him.

Well, one day, when I was in the box, waiting for confessions to start . . . it was a kind of slow Wednesday . . . a person came into the box, and started to talk. I knew it was the person whom I thought was dead. He said, "I came back to tell you not to worry. I'm all right," and then he left.

Well, I was amazed and really wanted to get out of the box. But I had to wait until he got out of the church. . . . I waited to hear the church door open and close. I waited a long time, but didn't hear the door. I really had to know . . . so I took a chance and stepped out of the box. But there was no one there.

I really think it was the person who committed suicide and he had come back to tell me he was okay, that I shouldn't worry any more. And now, everything really is okay.

A FRIEND of mine is a priest. He got up in the middle of the night and was wide awake. For some reason or another, he dressed and started to walk down the street with the idea of going to Holy Family Church which was some miles away.

As he was walking, he passed a park bench and saw a man sitting on the bench with his head down. He stopped and said to the man, "What's wrong?" The man said, "I'm on my way to end my life." The priest sat down on the bench and they talked until day break. He finally talked the man out of committing suicide.

God works his miracles in such mysterious ways!

✠ ✠ ✠

I NEVER COULD understand the Bible. No matter how much I read it, it never made much sense to me. Maybe it was because I tried to read the King James version . . . whatever.

I never understood it.

I worked at the post office . . . part of my duties were in the "lost and found" department. One day, a Bible appeared on my desk. I opened it and started to read it. It was a contemporary version of the Bible . . . and I really liked it. Reluctantly, I put it back in the lost and found department, figuring someone would claim it. But the next day, it was still there. I just opened it up and read some more. The Bible stayed, no one picked it up.

Finally, I took it home, put my name on it, and wrote in it, "A gift from God, 1986." And it truly was. I carry it with me every-where I go. It's changed my life!

✠ ✠ ✠

I AWOKE and this voice said, "Go and walk along the lake." I said, "It's thirty degrees along the lake; it's too cold." And the voice said, "Go and walk along the lake." I decided I'd better respond. So I walked down to the pier and as I stepped out on the pier, I slipped. I thought, "This is far enough—it looks dangerous." But the voice said, "Go to the end of the pier."

I walked carefully, step by step to the end of the pier. The sun was out. It was very cold. There were waves and birds and it was beautiful. Then, I heard a big *swoosh* and two kids, eighteen years old or so, jumped into the water. One swam to the sand bar, and the other one clung to the pier. I reached down to try to help him, but I couldn't pull him out. He was too heavy. I said to him, "You've got to swim." And he said to me, "I can't, my legs are frozen."

I looked around. Two guys were fishing off the pier. I called them over and they came and pulled him out. One guy who pulled him out said to the kid, "Get up and walk," and he did. Then he said to me, "Do you know these guys?" I said, "no." He said, "They must be drunk." I said, "Yeah, I guess." And he said, "Have a good day," and I went home.

How do I explain it? I don't know. I just know I needed to be there.

✙ ✙ ✙

(THE *young woman who shared this story called to tell us what happened to her after our meeting.*)

I JUST WANTED you guys to know that I've been healed! I never went to church . . . I didn't think about this sort of thing at all. Neither did my family. It just wasn't part of the way we grew up. It never seemed very important to me.

But I couldn't forget our meeting. And since that time, I just know I've been healed. I can't explain it. But I wanted you to know how good I feel. Everything's going really well.

It's pretty amazing!

✙ ✙ ✙

FIVE months ago, my husband died, leaving me with two small children. I was deeply depressed and having more and more trouble just getting through the day.

One day, I was in my bedroom and it felt like the room was being filled with light. It was a turning point in my grieving, but I didn't tell anyone because I thought they would think I was crazy.

But, now, I think I can tell people. It was a powerful healing experience. Thank you for helping me to trust and believe my experience.

✤ ✤ ✤

IN WORLD WAR II, I was trained to pilot an LST and was sent in the invasion of Normandy to Omaha Beach. The night before the invasion, we were given orders that we were to carry our sidearm and any man who refused to get off the LST was to be shot and killed.

The trip from the ship to the beach was hell. The water was red with blood. But I got to shore, beached the boat and dropped the front door. The men rushed out . . . there were bullets everywhere. Everyone left but the Protestant chaplain. He fell on his knees and would not leave the boat.

I said to him, "Get off the boat!" but he didn't pay any attention. I pulled out my sidearm and said, "I'll have to shoot you if you don't get off the boat. That's an order!" But he didn't move. He was paralyzed with fear. And I couldn't shoot him.

So I raised up the door, backed the boat off and turned around for the next load. I knew I was in deep trouble. Sure enough, in the next few days, I was brought up on charges to be court martialed. The charges were that I had disobeyed a direct order under fire. The penalty for that was death. There wasn't much argument about what had happened.

As I was standing in the room aboard the ship where the court martial was being held, and feeling like I was going to be standing in front of a firing squad pretty soon, suddenly the door opened and everyone turned and stood at attention. In came Admiral Kinkaid, who was Commander in Chief of naval operations.

He walked over to me and put his arm around me and said, "I've heard about this man and his story. And I want to tell you I would have done the same thing."

I was not sentenced at the court martial. I was free. I knew that this was God acting in my life."

CHAPTER 9. STORIES OF SPIRITUAL HEALING WITH PHYSICAL CURE

IT WAS a terrible shock when I got the news from my doctor that I had breast cancer. He said it was not an aggressive one, and so I decided to wait until the holidays were over before I had it removed. When my family heard the news, they decided to stay and help out, and my daughter, who lives in Florida, started a prayer chain in her church.

Finally, I went to the hospital. I was constantly checking my breast to feel the lump, which was quite a large one, and I was having a burning sensation in my breast. I was not happy with that new symptom, but put it down to stress. During that time, I also met with my pastor and he was very calming. I was able to pray, "Whatever you want for me, God, that's what it will be." When I prayed that prayer, I was engulfed by an overwhelming peace! It was very powerful.

An intern came into the room to check my breast the night before surgery and said, "Where's your lump? I can't find it." He decided that he was just tired and left. I didn't think too much about it. I was still feeling peaceful in spite of what was going to happen.

The next day, they prepared me for surgery. The surgeon came into the operating room and examined me. When he finished he said, "I can't feel the tumor. You'll have to go down to X-ray and get it imaged so I can get on with this." When I came back from X-ray, the doctor said, "I can't believe this. I'll do a biopsy, but I think we'll only remove some tissue. The lump is not there."

I was anesthetized and the biopsy turned out to be benign. That was fifteen years ago. The doctors would not discuss the case with me. But I knew I had been healed by prayer . . . by the prayer I was able to pray . . . and the prayers of others. The doctors wouldn't even listen to that. But I knew.

IN 1984, I suddenly collapsed. My husband drove me to the hospital and upon finding evidence of internal bleeding, I was put in an emergency operating room. During the course of the surgery, I "died" but was resuscitated. My husband was told I had a 10 percent chance to live out the night.

Immediately, he and the church set up prayer circles which spread to many churches. For fifty-three days, I was in the intensive care unit. I developed a whole bunch of complications: septicemia, toxic shock, you name it. But I survived. The doctor said to me, "Your healing is a miracle. It certainly was not in my hands."

My life is different now and I'm different. I feel less concerned about little things. But I do find myself asking, "Why me? Why did I survive?"

I WAS LIVING in a part of the world which had good medical attention, but not very much of it. I was four months pregnant when I discovered this big lump in my breast. I was really scared, and went to the local doctor who sent me to a top specialist in the city. The trouble was, I couldn't get in to see him for two weeks.

I was really worried about my children, not to mention the one on the way. What was I supposed to do? What if I died? I'm the only one to raise my kids. I prayed to God and I said, "I'm scared! What can I do, God? There's only me. What will my kids do if I'm not here? I'm really afraid."

And then I found myself saying, "But you do what you have to do, God. I trust you." And I was filled with a great peace. So much so that for the next two weeks, I didn't examine my breasts or even think about the problem while I had to wait.

When at last I saw the doctor, they could find no lump . . . the lump was gone.

"What did you do?" they asked. I told them, "I prayed."

The doctor did not know what to do with that, but he said, "Come back when the lump returns." But I said to him, "I will not be back. I am healed!"

When I saw my original doctor, he said to me, "Whatever happened, you did the right thing. I thought you were going to die!"

✢ ✢ ✢

WHEN I got my second diagnosis of ovarian cancer and was told the prognosis was very bad, I decided that I wanted to do a better job of dying than I had done with living. I prayed that prayer, asking God for help with my dying. But God said to me that I had to do a better job of living first.

I trusted God to show me what he meant. I have tried to be open to God, and have been working on that for the last sixteen years. Yes! My cancer is gone, even though it had metasticized into my bowel. My doctor says I am cured. I know I am healed.

The hard part of this good news is that I have lived through the death of friends who have had what I had and who have died. I guess I have survivor's guilt. . . . I say, "Why me?"

I visit with a group of women with ovarian cancer and it is very hard. I struggle with what it means to be open and with what to do next; what action I should take. The first thing that happened to me after my good news was starting a Stephen ministry. I didn't want to . . . I felt I had enough on my plate. But the minister said we were going to St. Louis to train and we did. I said yes. I know it was God's direction.

I HAD a friend who was in a prayer circle with me. She was terminally ill, but was also an active part of our circle. One day, she was praying for our minister when she felt a wash come over her whole body. She knew she was cured even though she wasn't praying for herself. She went to the doctor and he confirmed it.

I HAD a physical healing while I was in college. I didn't want to be there and was having a very tough time. I had all kinds of physical problems . . . hives, cystitis, tonsilitis . . . but still had a 4.0 average.

When I went home for Christmas, it was decided I should have my tonsils out. I was recovering when I started to hemorrhage and went into shock. I was rushed to the emergency room. But they couldn't stop the bleeding. I heard one of the nurses say, "She's not going to make it."

I was very weak, but I started to pray. I began to sing hymns to myself. I was really scared. Somewhere in all of this, I suddenly felt that everything was okay. A great calm and peace descended upon me. Suddenly, it didn't matter what happened . . . whether I lived or died, it was okay. I had let go of my fear.

I lived—and I learned the power of giving it all up to God.

✤ ✤ ✤

IN 1970, I was diagnosed with breast cancer. I was surprised because I felt okay and did not suspect anything was wrong. But in rapid-fire order, I was diagnosed, operated on, and received chemotherapy. I didn't have time to be scared. I prayed a lot and others prayed for me and I felt safe.

I survived it all and was on my way to a seven-year cure when, in 1975, the cancer recurred. It was devastating . . . there were no support groups for breast cancer patients then. I felt hollow and desperate inside. My children were too young to talk to and my husband was in denial . . . so he was no help. People didn't seem to want to talk about it. I was really isolated and alone.

I was told I needed heavy duty chemotherapy. I didn't want it. It made me so sick. I was told that I didn't have a choice. I became very depressed and felt betrayed by God. One morning, I awoke and just fell apart all over the place . . . emotionally . . . I was filled with anger and fear. I realized that my back was against the wall, and at that point I prayed for deliverance.

I went to the hospital alone for the chemotherapy; I didn't want my husband there. What I needed was a "sister," another woman to be with me. I called a friend who was a social worker. She was not really comfortable about cancer . . . she couldn't really support me. But she took the day off work and came to be with me.

My primary care doctor was late and during the time I waited, I prayed. He was part of a team that was working on another case. So a new doctor came in to see me. Another doctor in the room asked how he was and he said, "comme ci, comme ca." I recognized that answer as a kind of patois used in New Orleans where I grew up. I fell into conversation with him . . . he was from New Orleans. We talked, he held my hand, and it felt very good.

But as we talked, I started to hyperventilate . . . and then something happened! Something came from my heart. I gave a deep sigh . . . it was a sigh of relief. I knew I would be okay. I knew that I was cured. I felt renewed.

I left the hospital without doing any chemotherapy. I said to my friend, "I've been healed." She thought the doctor had given me good news and asked, "How do you know?" I said, "I just know I've been healed. The doctors haven't said anything." My friend pulled back from me, looking at me strangely. I said, "I can't explain it. I just know I've been healed."

I never went back to the clinic. That was in 1975. I am healed. I wanted to tell people about my experience, but they didn't want to hear it. It was hard to have this marvelous healing and nobody wanting to hear about it. I shut up and didn't talk about it.

But one night, I heard someone say that people should not ever stop trying to share what God has done for them . . . so I began to share it again.

Now my oldest daughter has breast cancer and I have shared this story with her. She has no medical insurance because her husband has been laid off after fifteen years. But my youngest daughter found a cancer program for uninsured women and now she is covered. I am not afraid for my daughter.

I am proclaiming my riches!

Rev. Bobbie McKay, Ph.D., and Lewis A. Musil, M.A.

I THINK my favorite word might be "fearlessness." Until a little while ago, I lived in great fear. I was claustrophobic . . . especially about elevators. It was so bad, I couldn't go on one unless there were other people on it too. If one came and I was alone, I would turn my back on it and pretend it had not yet come. I was truly a prisoner of my fear and my phobia.

Last August, I went to a church conference and someone read a scripture which I had heard a hundred times before . . . but never "heard" it. you know how that goes. The scripture said, "God has not created in us a spirit of fear."

Well, I really heard it this time. I turned to my friend and said, "I've been healed. Get me to an elevator! I can't wait to try it. I did, and it's no problem for me to this day.

WHEN I was sixteen, my mother had a cerebral hemorrhage. That was back in 1970 . . . they didn't have all the equipment that they do today. It was very serious. They didn't know if she could even survive the tests. They took a bunch of pictures of her brain and said they would have more information the next day.

I went home with my dad . . . we were very upset. He got drunk, and I had to put him to bed. I was only sixteen, and this seemed really heavy. I was in the habit of praying, so I got on my knees and prayed as hard as I could to God to heal my mother. As I was praying, I heard a voice saying, "All is well."

The next morning at the hospital, we met with the surgeon who was in scrubs and looked very grave. We all went down to the X-ray room. All the x-rays were there (there must have been a hundred of them) of my mother's brain. He picked up a pointer and said, "See this line here? This is scar tissue. I think this is where the aneurism was . . . I don't know what has happened . . . I don't know how to explain it. But it's gone."

This changed my life. I've had a hard time believing that God intervened in history. I thought God was more passive. But this led me to believe that God acts in the world . . . and that maybe, just maybe . . . we can have something to do with that.

TWENTY-SEVEN years ago, I was asleep and was awakened by a voice which said, "After the operation, you will be all right." Seeing as I was not sick, and there was no operation scheduled, I just put the whole thing down to some quirk and forgot all about it.

Sometime later, I was diagnosed with pancreatic cancer. I was told that there was an operation that might help. But the surgery was very risky and the chances of survival were almost zero. That didn't sound very promising. I had forgotten all about the voice. So I just desperately tried to control my recovery. I really didn't want to do the surgery. But I was depleted and going downhill fast.

I contacted a prayer group and we prayed together. The next day, the group served communion and somehow . . . I don't know how . . . during the communion I just let go. I said, "I can't do it." But I had lost forty pounds by this time and I knew at that moment that I had to say "yes" to all of it in order to survive . . . that meant looking at the option of surgery again. And I decided to do it.

From the moment I surrendered at that communion, my life has been a blessing. I survived the operation. I was okay and I slowly got better. Now every morning, I wake up and say,

"Thanks!" My life really started after the operation. The voice was right!

✤ ✤ ✤

I WAS on an Emmaus walk . . . It's a retreat experience . . . I had gone there even though my wife was in the hospital having follow-up tests to confirm the diagnosis of degenerative heart failure. They wanted to see just how bad her condition was. Anyway, she told me to go on the walk. It had been scheduled for some time. I didn't know what to do, but I decided it would be okay to leave her.

But on the walk, I was thinking about her all the time, and started to pray aloud for her. There were about fifty people in the group and they all joined in prayer with me for my wife. When I returned, the report we got was that she had a healthy heart. It really felt like a miracle.

✤ ✤ ✤

SEVEN YEARS AGO, I was in the locked ward of a mental hospital. My husband had divorced me and my kids were gone . . . both kids were addicts on the street somewhere. I was catatonic . . . just lying on my bed . . . it felt like returning to the womb. Everyone was giving up on me but I didn't care. It felt wonderful . . . comfortable . . . safe . . . warm . . . nothing to do, nothing to worry about . . . just being taken care of.

One day, I heard one of the doctors say that if they didn't get through to me in three days, they would lose me. I didn't care. What did I have to live for anyway?

That night, I was resting . . . partly sleeping, I guess . . . when the door opened, and I saw a figure standing in the light of the hallway. At first, I didn't know who it was . . . it didn't look like any of the doctors or people who worked in the hospital. Then I realized that it was Jesus standing there in the doorway. He looked at me and said, "Get up! You can't go yet. Your children need you." There was nothing meek or mild about that voice. It was tough, not nice at all. But I heard him, and I knew what I had to do.

The problem was that I was in a locked ward in a mental hospital. If I told the doctors that Jesus had come to me and told me to get up . . . well, I'm not sure I would ever have gotten out of the hospital.

But I did . . . I was able to convince them that I was all right. I was discharged. I went out and found my children and moved us all here. The kids are all right now—off drugs and straight. We're a family again.

This is the first time I have ever told this story. I was too afraid people would judge me or think I was really crazy . . . they wouldn't understand what happened to me. But I tell it now because my love for God is so strong now . . . I'm so strong now . . . that I want to share what happened to me.

I WAS in the hospital with my first child when they found I had a tumor. The pastor came by and asked me if I would like to pray. I said, yes, and every time he prayed with me, I felt something happening inside of me. I felt my spirit being healed. And after that, I felt a physical reaction. My tumor was gone. I can't explain it. No one could. This was my introduction to prayer. Before this, I was ignorant of the Bible and too busy to bother much with 'religion.'

After I left the hospital, I went on a trip to Chicago with my husband. I shopped around while he was busy and ended up in a book store. While just browsing, I found a book there about Saint Luke and Saint Paul. Without thinking about it, I bought it and went back to the hotel room, read the book, and went to bed.

When I awoke, I was simply not the same person. I changed from being highly opinionated . . . that was gone . . . my self-pride was gone. Instead, I felt acceptance and I felt forgiven. When we got back home, I went to church. In the service, we sang "Amazing Grace". . . the hymn just jumped off the page at me. It was a profound experience and I knew I was changed.

✤ ✤ ✤

MY HEALTH is not good . . . I have had several bouts with cancer recently. But before all that, I had a ruptured appendix. After the operation, I was in the ICU and the doctor said that he had not expected me to survive the surgery . . . I had several large blood clots which they could not reach and a deep infection which they thought was in my brain. They couldn't control it. They wanted to do a spinal tap, but I said, "No. I've had enough of that stuff." The doctors said I would probably die.

Now, I had been raised a Baptist, but I had thrown all that stuff out of my life. I was an agnostic, and that was just the way it was. I called my parents to come to the hospital because I didn't want to die alone. They said they could come the next day.

But then I thought, if I'm going to die, maybe I ought to pray. I went into the chapel and in that praying experience . . . I suddenly felt that my soul was cleansed and that I was going to be OK.

That night, at 2:00 A.M., I was lying in bed, staring at the ceiling. I saw a mist which descended on me and then I felt this low voltage electricity go through me. It swept from my head to my foot. I heard a loud voice that said, "Behold the Lamb of God which taketh away the sins of the world". . . . words I must have heard from my childhood experiences in church.

I broke into tears and cried all night. In that experience, I somehow knew I was being loved . . . but how could God love me when I was such a sinner?

The next day, before my parents arrived, they did a CT scan. They found that the blood clots were gone, along with the infection. I was healed.

I FELT I had a rough childhood . . . then I got married early and had an eight-month-old baby on my hands at the time that this happened. We were on our way to a funeral when we got to the top of a hill on a narrow road and met a truck coming fast. My husband swerved and so did the truck in such a way that it hit the passenger side of the car and pinned me in the front seat. I was part way in and part way hanging out of the car.

I was knocked out, and when I came to, I saw that I had my husband's head in my hands. It was disconnected from his body! I freaked out . . . and then I said to God, "I can't do anymore." And I passed out again.

When I came to the second time . . . I don't know if it rained or not . . . but the clouds parted and the sky was this glorious blue. I felt this surge of electricity . . . this surge of power all over and inside me. It got me through the ordeal of being rescued out of the wreck. It carried me through the long healing process. And it saved my baby . . . she was miraculously unhurt. She is forty two now and healthy. It was all God's actions that saved us.

THERE are a lot of problems in this life, I can tell you. People envy you and try to keep you down . . . and sometimes you get sick. Well, I had a lot of trouble with my coworkers. I was so stressed out that I was getting bad headaches every day. I wanted to see the doctor . . . tried to get an appointment . . . but I couldn't fit anything in with my work schedule.

One Sunday it was so bad I called the doctor at her home. She said, "What's wrong?" and I started to tell her my symptoms and she interrupted and said, "No! What's wrong . . . I don't mean the headaches . . . what's wrong?" I told her and we prayed together over the phone and . . . I was healed in that moment.

Then I prayed for the woman who was giving me so much trouble and she has changed! God is so good! God will get you through anything.

MY SON had been shot, and I followed the ambulance to the emergency ward. When I got there, they told me he was dead. I said, "I don't think so." I walked into a corner of the hospital and I said to God, "All my life I have believed in you. Now prove it to me!" I went back to the room where my son was, and the doctor said he was sorry but that my son was dead. And I said, "I don't think so."

I went over to the table, and I said to him, "okay, the doctor says you are dead, but I don't think so. So move your right arm." My son started to shake all over and I said, "Open your eyes." He couldn't do that, although you could see his eyes rolling under his lids. The doctor said that was natural with dead people, but I said, "I don't think so" and took his hand. I said, "Squeeze my hand," and he did. The doctor couldn't believe it.

My son not only survived, he now has two jobs. When you say there's nothing more I can do . . . then God can make it happen. He was paralyzed, but now he can work two jobs. I know God healed him.

MY SON had broken his neck. I was in shock . . . crushed . . . desperately afraid. About 3:00 A.M., I said to God, "I can't let go of him. But if that's what you want, then you will have to give me the strength to do it."

I felt a great peace and was able to give up my control of the situation . . . and my son was not only healed, he recovered fully.

I WAS DIAGNOSED with a three-centimeter tumor in my right breast. I asked Jesus to heal me. When they did the surgery, they found that the tumor was gone. Not only that, there were clean margins all around the site.

I fell in love with God!

MY SON had broken his neck. I was in shock . . . crushed . . .

I WAS DIAGNOSED with cancer of the kidney and the liver. I decided that I would put my trust in the Lord and that would be how I would handle it. People thought I was in denial because I was so sure I'd be okay. When they operated, they found that both tumors were nonmalignant. And I wasn't surprised.

But in the hospital, I saw a little boy who was truly dying of cancer. I thought, "Why me? Why was I saved?" I thought I had to do something to express the gratitude I felt, and to do something for others not as fortunate as I had been.

For some reason, quilts became the answer. I started making quilts for the McDonald houses that take care of sick children. A whole group of people formed around this. We felt surrounded with prayer and our group just bloomed. And we also made a lot of beautiful quilts to help a lot of sick children. We're still doing it.

✣ ✣ ✣

I HAD CANCER of the stomach and the prognosis was that I had only six months to live. I held hands with my prayer group and we prayed.

That was twenty-five years ago, and I'm still here praying and thanking God for God's miracles in my life and in the lives of others.

✣ ✣ ✣

I WAS LEAVING the parish to take a new church when I saw a woman I had worked with for five years. I apologized to her for being so ineffective in helping her situation. Her husband was an alcoholic and they were on the verge of a divorce. I just couldn't seem to find any way to help them.

But she assured me, "No, don't worry about it. You're my friend . . . you did what you could."

The day before I left, I saw the husband. He was having a drink and I said to him, without thinking about the power of my words, "Go ahead and kill yourself with alcohol. Maybe that will settle your problems." But for years I felt terrible about what I had said to him. And I felt guilty and worried about what he might have done with that advice.

Five years later, I happened to come back to that church for a visit. I was quite surprised to see them together and . . . happy. I was also relieved to see him alive and well. I found out later that after I had said what I said to him, he went home and took all the bottles he had and lined them up on the dresser. He knew it was life or death. Then he asked himself if he really wanted to live. And he said, "Yes!"

He said a prayer and dumped all the liquor down the sink. He called AA and went to a meeting. Six months later he asked his wife to put the divorce on hold. He started to court her again and was a changed man. Everything else was changed too.

I was so grateful to be used in this healing.

✣ ✣ ✣

MY HUSBAND was very ill . . . we were living in New Jersey. We had young children and he was facing serious cancer surgery. I felt all alone and didn't know what to do.

I went to the chapel at the hospital. I sat down and thought, What do I do now?

I sat there for a while, and then I said, "God, there is no way I can convince you to do what I want you to do. I want him to be well. But it's up to you . . . Please help me get through it and help the kids. I don't know your plan. Please just help me get through this."

He was totally cured. There were lots of prayer groups praying for him. But somewhere in the process, he knew there was a greater power at work for him. It changed him completely.

✣ ✣ ✣

MY WIFE and I always liked to go to religious conferences with another couple. At this particular time, my wife had gone to the dentist and he discovered that she had an oral cancer that needed immediate attention.

But we were scheduled to go to a religious conference. We talked about it and decided to go to the conference before she had to go to the hospital for oral surgery.

At the conference, we broke into small groups and one of them was a healing request group which my wife went to. She was able to ask for healing in her group. Then we went to the hospital and she went through a three hour surgical procedure.

At last, the doctors came out of the surgery and said to me, "We don't know what happened. We went in and checked everything and could find no cancer at all!"

I simply said, "Praise the Lord!"

✣ ✣ ✣

I HAD a good childhood and a good church experience when I was young. I continued to be a church person. When I was twenty-eight, my third son was pronounced dead after going into convulsions from taking some medication.

I was angry and refused to believe that God would take away my child . . . not quite two years old. In desperation, I went to the chapel in the hospital. When I was there, I experienced something . . . a presence that focused my prayer on God. I didn't know what it meant . . . what was happening. But I felt the anger going away from me, and I knew that I was in God's presence.

I had never experienced anything like this before. I was healed . . . reborn . . . but I felt I could say nothing about it to people at my church. I wasn't sure they would understand.

When I returned to my son's room, he was alive. It was a miracle gift from God. I realized this was a spiritual healing for me and for my son.

✣ ✣ ✣

WE WERE BUILDING a house for some people who had a new baby. We were almost done. We also held a prayer meeting every Saturday. On this particular Saturday, one of our members came to the meeting. He said he had heard that the new baby had fallen off a table and was badly injured. He didn't know more than that. So we started to pray for the baby.

Then the phone rang. It was the father of the baby and he said, "Are you guys having your prayer meeting?" We said, yes. He said, "Will you pray for him?" And of course we said, "Yes, we will." The child was dangerously close to dying. The father was crying hard.

Then we just knew what we had to do. We've got to go to the hospital. So we took off and at first we were so distracted we went to the wrong hospital. Then we got to the right place. We went to the ICU and sat for one half hour listening to the doctors talking about the baby. The baby looked awful. He had a skull fracture. The doctor said to us and his parents, "Don't expect anything, even if we can save his life."

We shared Scripture and then prayers. We knew the nurse was coming back soon and so we were ready to end our prayer when suddenly I got a pressure in my chest . . . as if there were something greater inside of me. My arm straightened out and I touched the child's head. I had no intention to do this. And I heard myself saying, "In the name of Jesus be healed." The child moved! Then his mother picked him up, he started to suck, and she nursed him. We left the hospital.

God has done his work really well. On Monday morning, the X-rays were normal. On Tuesday he went home from the hospital. He was cured. The doctors said, "This could not be the same child!"

We knew it was absolutely God's action that had saved him.

Rev. Bobbie McKay, Ph.D., and Lewis A. Musil, M.A.

✤ ✤ ✤

I HAD TO heal myself from alcohol, anger, and jealousy. If we buy into our bitter feelings, it makes us sick. I know this to be true.

Some time ago, my son's appendix ruptured. We took him to the hospital and they hooked him up to all those machines. He said to me, "Dad, it really hurts. Please pray for me."

I put my hand over his appendix and started to pray. I left around midnight after he fell asleep and went back to the motel. When I got back to the hospital the next morning, he was sitting on the edge of the bed, fully dressed, and ready to go home.

The doctor said, "I don't know what happened. His appendix was ruptured, but now there is no evidence of it."

It was a spiritual healing . . . I knew that. I can't explain it. He's just fine.

✤ ✤ ✤

I WAS WORKING in surgical intensive care, and a boy was sent to us that the surgeons couldn't help. He had been so badly beaten up on the head that they couldn't stop the bleeding. They just put a bunch of gauze inside and sewed him up. They took him to the ICU to die because they don't like people dying in surgery. They told me to run a slow code on him . . . let him die.

His family wanted to come in and see him. And although we don't like families there . . . since I was the one working, I let them in. I'm not sure they were Christians . . . but they had some kind of holy oil and they anointed him all over his body. I stayed out of the way and then they left. I waited for him to die. There didn't seem to be any hope.

I can't explain it . . . but he lived. There's no question that it was a healing . . . a true miracle.

MY FRIEND was diagnosed with breast cancer. She had a mastectomy and then the other breast developed cancer, and she was given a death sentence. She went to another doctor and got a course of chemotherapy. But while she was doing the chemotherapy, she decided to do something else . . . she went to a healing priest.

At that encounter with the priest, she felt something . . . couldn't explain more . . . but she knew something happened. That was years ago . . . her cancer was gone and she is still cancer free today. She was cured and healed.

MY SON was very ill. He came home from New Orleans. He had lost weight. He went to the VA hopsital where they checked him for cancer. But there weren't any signs of it. In fact, they just didn't know what it was. He had a large knot on his chest. They did an isotope angiogram and decided they had to do surgery to find out what was really wrong.

At 7:00 the next morning, I went to see him. All the doctors were there and they looked at me and said, "The knot is gone. We don't understand—it was there yesterday."

I said, "I understand . . . we prayed for him . . . as a matter of fact, the whole church did. It's a miracle."

MY SON, at the time of this story, . . . well he was four years old. He would come home from nursery school and he would say to me, "momma, do you know what?" And I would say, "What." and he would say, "God loves me!"

Well, I was having female problems and was going to have to have surgery. I needed to tell my son I would have to go to the hospital and be away from him . . . that I needed surgery . . . and try to prepare him for the fact that I might not come back. But I kept putting it off. I felt guilty about that . . . but I was also worried about whether I would survive the surgery. I knew for sure that I didn't want to die. I told my momma that she should make sure they used extraordinary measures if they needed to . . . and if they pulled the plug, she should put it back!

Three days before I went to the hospital, as I was taking my son to meet the school bus, he said to me, "Momma, I had a dream last night about God." And I said, "Really" . . . trying to help him put his coat and hat on. He looked at me, and he said, "Yes. I had a dream about God and God talked to me." I didn't know what to say, so I said, "What did God say?" My son said, "God told me to talk to you and tell you not to worry. Just hold out your hand to Jesus and Jesus will heal you."

Well, I didn't know what to do. But I sent him off to school. The day was very gloomy and dark, and I was very worried. When my son came home from school, he said, 'Momma, do you remember what I told you?" I said, "Yes, I remember." And finally I was able to tell him . . . "I've got to go to the hospital for an operation." But I told him I'd be back.

I went to the hospital, had the surgery, and found that the tumor was benign. I came back home and things got back to normal. But my healing was not the benign tumor. My healing was that my life has changed completely! I am really changed.

✤ ✤ ✤

THIS STORY involved our whole congregation. A little boy in the congregation was diagnosed with leukemia. He received a bone marrow transplant, and his mother e-mailed everything that was going on to every member of the congregation. It allowed us to connect with the family and offer continuous prayers.

He's doing very well now and the wonderful part was that everyone could participate in his healing. It really bonded our congregation in a special way. It's still a very important part of who we are.

MY STORY of healing deals with finally meeting someone who really cared. I am one-half Native American and was diagnosed with an incurable cancer. I had chemo, radiation, the whole nine yards. I was told, essentially, to go home and die. I was only concerned with my health and wrapped up in what was going to happen to me.

And then I found a Native American M.D. and she did some radical interventions—some herbs, etc. She said that my disease was a war, a spiritual war going on in me. The community took me in. There were group prayers and no matter how much I wanted to, they would not let me give up.

I finally trusted the powers that be and became determined not to die. I won! I was healed.

I LIKE to run, but I don't necessarily like to run with a lot of people around. So I try to find places that are quiet and remote. I was running on one of them where very few people ever came.

Suddenly, my heart began to fibrillate and I passed out. Two other runners happened to be running in this same place, which was very rare. They saw me on the ground and stopped. One of them ran to call 911 and the other tried to do CPR, but he didn't know how. He had never been trained.

He said that while he was trying to figure out what to do to save my life, he looked up and suddenly another man was there—a stranger. He said, "I don't know how to do CPR or anything." The stranger said, "I do. I'll tell you."

The CPR saved my life. But there were actually three gifts that day. The first gift was that there were any other runners around me in the first place. The second gift was that the ambulance guys were the best in emergency management in the area.

But the best gift, of course, was the stranger who told the man how to save my life. The man told me that when the ambulance guys started to arrive, he looked up to thank the stranger and he had disappeared. I tried to find him to thank him, but he was nowhere to be found.

For me it was a powerful healing. It saved my life.

CHAPTER 10. STORIES OF SPIRITUAL HEALING WITHOUT PHYSICAL CURE

I WAS a witness to a healing. My father was a strong man who was impatient . . . a workaholic and a real "doer." He was a minister and he spent a great deal of energy getting things right for the church.

Then, he had a heart attack which left him blind and disabled. He was given six months to live. But he lived sixteen years. From this affliction, he made an amazing transition to becoming accepting of his limitations. He assumed a different form of ministry, becoming a spiritual advisor and counselor to people. His impatience was replaced with patience and acceptance and he was able to do this because God had given him the "gift" of his affliction. That is the way he described it. It was truly miraculous.

I was deeply affected by the change in him and decided to go into the ministry as a result of what happened to him. This was a complete change of course for me. We were both healed . . . each in our own way.

Rev. Bobbie McKay, Ph.D., and Lewis A. Musil, M.A.

WHEN I was in Harvard Business School, I learned one of my professors was dying of cancer. I hesitated . . . not knowing if I should talk to him about it or not. But I decided to bring the subject up to him. He talked to me about his problem and thanked me for asking because he had found that he could not always talk to people about it. They simply didn't want to listen.

Listening can be healing . . . it can heal into life or into death. Either way.

I realize that God is God and I am not . . . and that has helped me to be healed myself.

(The setting for this story was in a room which was filled with beautiful photographs, all taken by the teller of the story . . . who also happened to be blind.)

IN 1991, I was told that I had a terminal illness and was given six to twenty-four months to live. I was a successful top corporate executive . . . type "A" person for sure. I cared nothing for anything other than myself . . . my pleasure and my power. I was only for me . . . self-absorbed totally.

In the face of this disease, my life has miraculously turned around. I recognized the truth of the Gospel and was transformed. I was so egocentric and self-centered. But since I have become blind . . . it's strange . . . somehow now all the women that I meet are beautiful and all the men are good-looking . . .

I can only tell you how grateful I am for my disease because it has transformed my life. Even though the gospels have been there all along, they were new to me. I am a different person.

And finally, today, I can share with you what I have been afraid to share. I am dying of AIDS . . . and I know you will not judge me. I couldn't share it before our meeting today.

✣ ✣ ✣

SOME of the things we do normally are quite healing . . . like what happened in August when my mother called me and told me that my father had stomach cancer. I saw him the day before his surgery . . . he was on a dozen different prayer chains . . . all praying for him.

Anyway, he had the surgery and then got the report which was not good. The cancer had metasticized and he was given three to six months to live. When he went back to the hospital and the doctor told him the news, he said, "I guess that means I'll get to heaven sooner than I expected."

He and all of us had prayed for a cure. But he had gotten a healing instead.

✣ ✣ ✣

EVERYONE thinks the pastor has it all together. Well, this church has shaped my theology, particularly through two experiences. One experience was about intercessory prayer, and the other one about healing services.

After considerable wrestling with the problem about my son, I finally became willing to make an intercessory prayer for him. He has muscular dystrophy. I felt that God knew all about the problem anyway so I had never prayed for my son. It didn't seem necessary.

I talked to our prayer group about this and they insisted that I should make an intercessory prayer for him. I have had many hopes for my son, but I had just buried them. But I went along with the prayer group and I prayed that he would find a girlfriend. I knew that would be so helpful to him. I didn't have any hopes that it would happen. Incredibly, he found a girlfriend, and is happily married. The healing was for me.

THE OTHER experience I had was about healing services. I was reluctant to start a healing ministry and I would not lay hands upon people because I didn't want them to think that I had any healing power. However, the prayer group at church insisted that we have healing experiences. They persuaded me to try it.

I went to a woman's home from the congregation who had serious cancer and who had asked for anointing with oil. There were eight people there for the healing service and I had exactly enough communion elements to do the service.

I came back later to see her and she told me that she did not expect to be cured. But now she knew that she was healed! She taught me about healing.

I HAVE a friend who is close to seventy, whom I have known for twenty years or so. He was born with cerebral palsy . . . he used to say that he was the runt of the litter. Well, his hands shook all the time. But he learned to walk and get around. He educated himself and went to church. He made a fundamentalist connection . . . but he was not a member of any one church. He was always traveling somewhere.

He built log cabins—log houses for a living, as well as doing all sorts of carpentry. He also did a lot of writing. But he wasn't happy. He always wanted to be cured of his shaking hands. He looked all over for someone to cure him . . . but no luck. No one could cure him.

One day in Louisiana, he was helping a pastor put a new roof on the parsonage. He was working away, climbing all over the roof, and he asked the pastor why he was never healed.

The pastor said, "Look at your life . . . what do you want from it? You have cerebral palsy. And yet here you are up on this roof pounding nails . . . you are making it. What else do you want God to do?"

And then he knew that he would not be cured of his shaking. But he also knew that he was healed.

I HAD A HEALING when my friend got pancreatic cancer. I was angry and very unhappy and resentful about it. It wasn't fair. But I also knew that I would be with my friend . . . we would do this together. And we did, and we became very close.

One day, as I was walking with her to the CT scan, I suddenly realized that if this awful thing had not occurred, we would never have taken the time to get this close. I still hated the situation, but I know we both had experienced some kind of healing.

I'VE HAD terrible eyes all my life, but God has always restored what little vision I have, whenever it is threatened. I had a corneal transplant a short time ago, and it was wonderful for a while. But then it started to reject . . . it got really bad and I was terribly down . . . I could hardly work.

One day at work when I was not too busy, I decided to clean out my cupboard. I found an old braille copy of *Guideposts* . . . it must have been two years old. I picked up this article about a baseball player who had cancer in his arms. He had worked his way back so he could pitch again in the majors.

But in his first game, his arm shattered and he was unable to play. He was devastated, but finally he realized that God had given him a miracle, and that a miracle lasts forever! The article hit me like a bolt of lightning. I read it over and over again.

My eye is improving a little . . . we don't know what that will mean. But I know I was healed before that happened.

I AM a severe diabetic and am nearly incompetent. I can just barely move around. One day, I was sitting in a chair and moved the wrong way. The chair fell over and trapped me. I couldn't move. I was really trapped. I hollered for help, but there was no one around. I didn't know what to do. I was really helpless.

After a while, I heard a knock at the door. I yelled, "Come in!" and a couple I had never seen before walked in. They helped me up and got me settled. They were total strangers.

They said they had been driving around town and both felt this intense need to come to my house. They felt that someone needed help, and they decided to respond, even though they couldn't understand what was happening.

It was a real miracle in my life . . .

IN SEPTEMBER of 1982, I broke my hip. They pieced it back together, put me in traction. There I was, lying in this absurd situation. I was in a double room . . . but after a few days, they moved my bed over to the window.

I had been trying to pray about my situation. But I didn't seem to make much headway with it. But one evening, looking at the sunset, I was engulfed by a feeling of peace. It was the peace that passes all understanding. I knew that I would be okay.

It didn't cure me . . . I couldn't get up and walk . . . but I know I was healed. And I know it was that feeling of peace that changed everything.

MY SON was diagnosed with cancer and died in seventy-seven days. I was in touch with him every day . . . I prayed . . . did it all. It was no use. After he died, I said to God, "I did everything you told me to do. You said you would heal him, but you didn't."

And God said to me, "But I did." And then I thought . . . I remembered all the trouble he had had in this life. It really was a hard life for him all the time. And now, he was healed of all of that. This was my introduction to spiritual healing.

THIS COMMUNITY has helped me to consider spiritual healing again. This is the twentieth anniversary of my husband's death at age forty-six. He had a viral cardiomyopathy and was just slipping away. After six months of suffering, he was given a new heart and lived one more year.

In that year, we traveled all around the country, thanking all the people who had helped us. As we traveled around, we felt so blessed to have this time together to do what we were doing. It was a healing for both of us.

When he died, I did not have to mourn.

MY HEALING is a work in progress. But it's taken an awful long time to work out all the negatives. First, my father died. But before that, I had been so hurt, so injured by him . . . in every way you could be hurt. I always thought I would never get over it. But I'm slowly coming to terms with that.

My mother was an alcoholic . . . no help there. I was date-raped and considered killing myself. But I am beginning to realize that scars are beautiful because they are a sign of healing.

The amazing thing is that somehow I have made it . . . that God saw something in me that was worthwhile. And God did something for me. God healed me. It fills me with such a sense of wonder. It is God, not me, who does all the healing.

I WORK in a hospice and see a lot of people healed before they die. I had problems of my own . . . I had a large brain tumor.

One day, while sitting at my desk, I suddenly felt I had collapsed into the arms of God. I knew whether I lived or died, I was with God. The outcome of my disease lost its significance, and from that time on, I've had a good time.

It's all true. God is here . . . holding us all the time.

I HAD a friend who was a "princess." She was beautiful but only interested in how she looked . . . you know the type. Then she got leukemia and everything changed. The chemotherapy was very hard on her . . . she lost her looks and became very depressed.

Then she came across a piece of scripture, "Make of your body a living sacrifice . . . be ye transformed." And it changed her. She has recovered from her early preoccupation with her looks, etc., and she's getting married.

She doesn't know how long she'll live, but she knows that each day is a gift. She has healed all of us.

I THOUGHT you might appreciate this story. One year ago, I was in the hospital waiting for a liver transplant. It felt like a very strange time. Here I was, waiting for someone else to die so that I could have a part of their body in order to live myself. All I could do was to wait and hope . . . and pray that I would live long enough to receive the transplant. But each day, I felt a little worse and a lot more anxious and frightened.

My wife and I had recently joined a church but we didn't really know anyone there. So we felt very alone in this waiting period.

But one day a get-well card arrived from the church. I was really surprised. It was the kind of card that says we're thinking about you and praying for you. And as I held the card, I felt an immediate sense of peace. I can't explain it. I was just holding the card, and I began to feel different. The waiting became bearable. It was a real turning point for me . . . this sense of peace when nothing else had changed.

Shortly after I received the card, I also received my new liver. I haven't rejected it yet . . . and I may. But I will always remember that sense of peace. It was remarkable!

I WAS surprised and unhappy when I found out that our son was diagnosed as "dyslexic." In trying to find out more about dyslexia in order to help my son, I discovered that both my daughter and myself were mildly dyslexic. That led me to look back into the family's past and found that there was dyslexia in preceding generations.

About that same time, I found a book that I think was called The Gift of Dyslexia. And, through our experiences and the book, I began to see that we were all bonded together in a very special way and that it was not a problem as much as it was a "gift." The letting go of dyslexia as a problem and embracing it as a gift was a real healing for all of us.

✛ ✛ ✛

MY HEALING was in the form of an understanding between me and a young man of my age who was dying of leukemia. In the course of becoming his doctor, I also became his friend. We did not specifically talk about Jewish things. But the last time I saw him before he died, he took my hand and said, "Thanks for taking care of me."

I helped him, but he uplifted me. It was a healing without a cure.

The Stories: An Afterword

YOU MAY have noticed that in a world where many spiritual stories are being told, the ones we've presented here are some-what different. The difference lies in the nature of our inquiry and the question asked: "What stories do you tell which fit your definition of spiritual healing?" Hence, our collection of stories was not gathered to inspire or reassure or make us feel better (though all these things happened in our sessions and may well have happened to you as you read them), but rather to define the moment of the occurrence, the actual healing experience.

The important thing in our population was not what happened after the moment, but the moment itself, which changed and transformed the lives of the people experiencing it. Except in the cure of disease stories, nothing on the outside of our population may have changed very much, if at all. But the change within the person continued to manifest itself to this very day, sometimes in subtle and sometimes in not-so-subtle ways.

Their story then was not just the one recalled of the moment of knowing the presence or action of God in their lives, but their lives themselves, lived out from the moment of change. Their future actions proceeded from this moment, this center filled with the unforgettable and indelible presence of God.

PART III

WHAT WE'VE LEARNED AND WHAT YOU CAN DO

CHAPTER 11.   WHAT WE'VE LEARNED FROM PEOPLE IN THE STUDY

WHEN WE FIRST envisioned this project, we were aware that the words "Spiritual Healing" formed a very ambiguous phrase. . . . It was that very quality of ambiguity that prompted us to start the project in the first place. After all, this phrase was being used in one way or another in a wide variety of social and scientific contexts. Perhaps it was time to see what it really meant to people who claimed to have had such experiences, particularly in the church, which seemed unusually quiet on the subject.

This was the core of our approach: to see what people in religious communities, involved in the process of spiritual healing, meant by it. . . . We did not want to use predetermined categories which we might validate statistically, nor opt for one point of view as opposed to another. We did not want to do a review of the literature. . . . We just wanted to see what people meant when they talked about the words, "spiritual healing."

People Really Are Interested in the Subject
The first thing we learned from the project was that the subject

of spiritual healing was of considerable interest. The conventional wisdom of the church as expressed to us was that no one would be particularly interested in spiritual healing. Our 96% positive response rate from our letter asking churches to participate in the project certainly contradicted this "wisdom." While we cannot know what was in the minds of the pastors to whom we directed our letter as to what they thought we would do or what the experience might be like, it is clear they were interested enough in the subject to take a chance on two strangers coming into their church and asking questions. The fact that we were strangers and did not represent ourselves as "experts" in spiritual healing also helped to guarantee the purity of the response: it was clearly a response to the subject and not to the presenters.

A significant number of people attended the sessions. The groups ranged in size from one to two hundred, the average being about twenty in the United Church of Christ churches and fifteen in the Catholic churches. The age of the participants ranged between twenty and eighty, with the biggest group in the forty-to sixty-year range. Our sample was predominantly from the United Church of Christ (101 churches). The total number of Catholic churches participating in the project was eleven. Data from the Jewish Temples, as of this printing, is insufficient to know what the average attendance will be. Over twenty-four hundred people have already participated in the project.

Experiences in Sharing Spiritual Healing Stories

As we met with people, we found a possible reason for the expressed lack of interest in spiritual healing at the institutional level. Most participants told us that though they had had experiences of spiritual healing, they had not talked very much about this subject prior to our meeting and certainly had not shared

Rev. Bobbie McKay, Ph.D., and Lewis A. Musil, M.A.

their experiences in church. In fact, the church may be low on the list of places where people feel free to talk about spiritual healing.

People are reluctant to talk of their experiences for a variety of reasons. But most did not feel that the church was necessarily a safe place to talk about it, even though they understood Jesus' healing experiences to be a central part of his ministry. Parenthetically, a number of people told us that it was much easier to talk of "spiritual things" in their AA meeting or other twelve-step programs than in the church.

Our meeting was frequently described as the first time people had talked of their experiences. The most frequent reasons given for not sharing their stories were being thought "crazy", or "too religious" by other church members by which they appeared to mean being seen as a "born-again" Christian or "fundamentalistic" in belief.

When they became comfortable in the meeting, you could not stop them sharing their experiences. This was probably assisted by Bobbie's skills as a psychologist in creating a climate of trust. It also may have occurred due to the fact that we were strangers who would pass out of their lives at the end of the session. But the desire to tell their stories seemed to transcend even these considerations. People really wanted to share their stories, given the right situation.

Spiritual Healing as the Action or Presence of God

What most people were telling us was that they were experiencing the action or presence of God in their lives. At first, we were struck by the similarity of the words used to describe the spiritual healing experience. But as we heard the stories, we found that they also bore a marked similarity. From a state of upset, fear, anxiety, or sometimes a state of no strong effect, there was a sudden, uncontrolled change of state, a *transformation*, which was most often characterized as a deep sense of peace. This peace was not some emotional feeling of ease, but related to "the peace that passes all understanding." It had components far beyond ease and lack of tension.

This transformation and peace did not mean that they felt everything else would somehow change miraculously. Nor did it do so in most cases. But instead, they felt changed and they continued to be aware of the change in themselves long after the initial experience. The experience frequently became a benchmark by which they measured their lives. Every time we heard stories of spiritual healing it was clear that it was the same experience for people regardless of their ethnic, socioeconomic or geographic location.

The intensity of the experience lasted from a few seconds (or less) to a much longer time. But the memory of the experience, as related in a story about the experience, could reinvoke it and it was clearly not forgotten. The core experience seemed to cease when the person experiencing it tried to "get a hold" of it or tried to explain it. When they started to become aware of what was happening, instead of experiencing it, being a part of what was happening, it tended to slide away. But, not only did they remember the experience (frequently in vivid detail), the feeling or sense of the experience was also recaptured. The telling of the stories was frequently accompanied by tears. But these were tears of the depth of the experience, not tears of sadness.

Although there was effect in the telling, the stories were remarkably free of psychological material, although we did not request that it be absent. There were no psychological explanations or histories given. It was remarkable to note that others in the group did not use psychological terms in reacting to the stories, nor were advice and evaluation given. These stories and the core experiences of the stories were change and transformation, not release from psychological bondage.

The Validity of our Results

The randomness and diversity of our sample was important in establishing the validity of our results. The cross-cultural and cross-economic nature of the study might well have led to a variety of answers to the question, "What do you mean by the words: spiritual healing?" From the standpoint of race, class, and geographic diversity, conventional wisdom might have predicted different responses from different groups along some lines or other.

The uniformity of response, in all the diversity of our study, demonstrated an amazing agreement as to the meaning of the words in the lives of the participants. None of the groups would have had difficulty understanding the meanings and experiences of any other group because they were nearly the same.

The Element of Surprise and the Issue of Control

The element of the unexpected was common to most of the stories. The experience came as a surprise, an unexpected gift. This was particularly true in the stories which did not involve disease. Many of the cure stories involved addressing the problem of the disease in a variety of ways before the cure was present (e.g. prayer, healing services, etc.). However, even a number of those stories involved surprise at the outcome of the circumstances surrounding the outcome. In the nondisease stories, surprise was an even stronger motif. The element of surprise was closely linked to another issue: *the giving up of control.*

Unlike other disciplines in which attempts at control of self or other elements leads to a spiritual experience, the individuals we met found the experience marked by the "letting go" of control. It was frequently mentioned in many stories (and certainly implied in almost all of them) that the experience came after consciously letting go of trying to control the outcome of the situation. What, in fact, most people did was to pray the Gesthemane prayer in some form or another. Just as Jesus expressed his need ("Let this cup pass from me") and his obedience to God ("Yet, not my will, but yours be done,") so was that prayer mirrored in many of the stories.

It must be stressed, however, that simply praying to let go of the outcome was not a talisman for achieving the state of spiritual healing. It was not a method that could be used to ensure results. For many people, letting go came only after persistent efforts to achieve the results they sought had failed, leaving no apparent strategies except to turn the situation over to God's control. This leads to the overriding experience stated in each of the stories: *spiritual healing was not in the control of the individual. Spiritual healing was a gift from God.*

It must be remembered that our population was predominantly drawn from the Christian church and so these findings are more definitive of the Christian experience of spiritual healing, as opposed to other religions or more secular spiritual pursuits. Whatever the stance of these other ways, the experience seems to be rooted in this essential fact: *Spiritual healing is a free gift and it cannot be "purchased" by some action of ours.*

There are, of course, a galaxy of activities that legitimately surround spiritual healing. Among them would be prayer, reading of scriptures, study groups, prayer groups, worship, healing services, etc. But in the experiences we encountered, none of these additional activities could be relied upon to automatically produce a spiritual healing.

Experiences Within the Meetings

In the meetings themselves, another component of the process became clear. These experiences required both *telling and listening.* When people could *share the story* and *name the experience* as "spiritual healing" or the "action of God," etc., it helped to "make sense" of what had happened to them. The telling of the story revalidated the experience and reignited the heart of the teller as well as validating it for others.

But finding a forum to tell the stories was a problem as we have already noted. Generally, the telling of the story was reserved for a few (if any) carefully chosen people. The telling of the story in a larger context was simply deferred until a "safe" place became available to do so. For many, we presented the first "safe" place they had found in which to share their experiences. What that meant, of course, was that the story had been held deeply within one's consciousness and the necessary validation of sharing was not available.

One of the things that happened frequently in our meetings was the "Aha!" experience when someone realized that they, too, had had a spiritual healing after hearing it defined by another telling his/her story. The amount of ambiguity surrounding these experiences in the abstract and in popular thought is so daunting that many people are put off even thinking about them as possibly being part of their own lives. Or they feel that it is an esoteric, special experience available only for initiates. However, when others who were generally known to them shared their experiences, the ambiguity disappeared and spiritual healing became a possibility in their lives. The sharing of the stories in this context is a critical opening experience.

Another complete surprise for us was the number of times that people reported that they felt "healed" simply by attending the meeting. This was a response we heard in almost every church. We knew how much we were moved by the words and stories being shared. But because we had not expected this outcome, it was always a special surprise when we heard that the meeting itself was a healing experience for the participants.

There was also a general reluctance expressed for the meeting to end, even though people had been sitting without a break for over two hours. On one occasion, we had been rescheduled at the last minute to a later time. When we arrived in the late afternoon, we were told that the group had been in church, in one way or another, since 8:30 that morning. We despaired of even getting their attention in these circumstances. But we found such energy generated as they told their stories, we could hardly get away after spending close to three hours with them.

Corollary to this was our experience when we retold some of our stories to others in informal conversation about the project. Many times people would say on parting, "You know, I can't tell you why, but I feel better." This leads us back to the map man in our early travels who told us that not only did spiritual healing happen all the time, and was happening at that moment, but that he "felt better" as we talked about it.

Speculation as to why this happens is not part of our database. But we tend to think that maybe when people tell us of their spiritual healing experience in the now, it suddenly makes it seem a present possibility, not a future one. It allows us to see that "it" might happen to us. Most religion and religious training is curiously future oriented. We *will go* to heaven, we *will be* perfected. Whatever the language, there is a kind of general assumption on the part of many people that God's promises are future events.

Rev. Bobbie McKay, Ph.D., and Lewis A. Musil, M.A.

The action of telling the story roots the events in the now and that changes the experience for many of us. When these events occur and are shared, the thing that is shared is the amazing presence and love of God. That makes people feel better indeed.

Spiritual Healing as a Commonplace Event
Generally speaking, we heard stories of physical cure and stories of other kinds of healing. In our study, we heard many more stories of spiritual healing that did not involve the presence of disease than stories about physical curing through spiritual healing. This seems to go against the common idea that spiritual healing means the cure of a disease. What we found was quite the opposite. Most of the stories of spiritual healing we heard had no disease component at all. If you look at these stories in particular, they become commonplace events occurring often in life, or as our map man would say, "happens all the time." It is perhaps this universal fact that makes it hard for some people to identify them as examples of spiritual healing because they represent ordinary events in the lives of ordinary people.

Many of the stories did not relate to major crises or desperate situations. Instead, they dealt with everyday occurrences. A friend calls on the phone and the right word is spoken. A chance meeting occurs where healing takes place, etc. This commonplace quality of spiritual healing occurrences may cause people to misidentify them because they think that spiritual healing must be unusual and miraculous. The identification in the gospels of healing events as miraculous tends to give them a specialty which is, in our experience, unwarranted.

The Clergy and Spiritual Healing
The response of the clergy was interesting. More Protestant

clergy attended the meetings than Catholic clergy. However, the Catholic clergy were more forthcoming about their own spiritual healing experiences than the Protestant clergy. Our sample in the Jewish community is too small to speculate about Jewish clergy at this time.

There was some reserve manifested by both Protestant and Catholic clergy about the subject. A small number of the clergy hold or have held some kind of healing services. These ranged from irregular meetings to quarterly and, in one case, weekly healing services. The weekly service was led by a clergyman who was dying of cancer.

The reserve on the part of the clergy is understandable from several standpoints. First, many people associate spiritual healing with fundamentalistic or charismatic movements with which the mainline church has historically had some discomfort. Second, the experience of spiritual healing is not a process which can be controlled or even easily approached, for as we have had reported to us, trying to control the process interferes with or stops it. This lack of control can also be a problem to both clergy and institutions because part of the reason they exist is to help define what our spiritual life should be, which is a way of controlling it.

This is also reflected in the life of the clergy themselves who are often overwhelmed with what might be called the "business" or "housekeeping tasks" in the church. One of the parishes we interviewed had ten thousand members and only three full-time and two part-time priests. The amount of time available for extra undertakings in these circumstances is severely limited.

One of our clergy attendees summed up the problem in a letter she wrote to us after we had been at her church:

"On a personal note, I quickly found myself (you will not be surprised) totally engaged as much more than just a staff person. I realized, once again, that the busyness of my ministry has once again overwhelmed that awareness, that expectancy, that I used to have more readily at hand as I awaited those moments of insight and revelation that have been a part of my life's journey.

"Logically, I know that ministers need support systems and communal spiritual nurture, but that we tend to fall behind as the work of ministry takes over again.

"Thank you for the reminder that I can find my way back again to that renewed sense of the presence of God. I long for a continuation of what we lived the other night—just as surely as anyone else there.

"And I say that with a smile on my face and a wonderful sense of contentment and commitment."

The Language of Spiritual Healing

Although we visited far more Protestant churches than Catholic churches or Jewish temples, the fact that we were able to match ethnic and socioeconomic diversity for the Christian groups allows us to generate results with good reliability. We expect to find a similar diversity in our Jewish congregations as well.

The words shared by all groups were remarkably similar. The word "peace" was expressed in each Protestant and Catholic church as definitive of the experience of spiritual healing, as it was in the Jewish temples we visited. In fact, one would have been hard pressed to distinguish a list of Protestant words from their Catholic and Jewish counterparts.

The stories also reflected similar thematic material in each tradition. Occasionally, a Catholic story can be identified by a reference to one of the traditions of the church, e.g., the sacrament of penance, or a reference to a priest. But overall, one would have a difficult time differentiating between the stories on the basis of theological differences.

Perhaps the most exciting outcome from our research was our experience of a *natural interfaith experience* that was powerful and unexpected. We believe that the experience of sharing spiritual healing stories is such a deep connector between people that it is able to overcome barriers and boundaries in a unique way. The great unifying fact that emerged clearly in our study is that we are all one in the Spirit, regardless of our religious convictions, our ethnic or socioeconomic status, our gender, or our geographical location. The distinctions and divisions between people that are so frequently made in our world today simply did not appear in the words and stories of any participants.

In our study, differences blurred as we focused our attention on the action and presence of God in the world. The felt healing in that experience was a bond that transcended words but which was clearly understood and acknowledged. No longer separated by our external differences, we were spiritually joined by our common experience of healing. This was a *natural interfaith experience* of the highest order which flowed simply and directly from the acknowledged action and love of God, as expressed in people's lives.

The uniqueness of this experience allows for the transcendence of the divisions between us. But at the same time, it *preserves* our separate traditions. In the sharing of spiritual healing stories, we remove the fences between us in order to celebrate our individual religious heritage. Nothing is lost and real dialogue becomes a viable possibility.

We believe that the spiritual bonding which occurs in the sharing of spiritual healing stories would provide a similar interfaith thrust between other divergent groups of people. For it is God's actions that are being shared, and not simply the

Rev. Bobbie McKay, Ph.D., and Lewis A. Musil, M.A.

expressed differences between people. In that context, the concentration and attention is focused on the loving actions of God for all people, creating a universal language that knows no limitations. In the chaotic and divided world in which we live, this is an opportunity for healing that we ignore at our peril.

In Conclusion

The data from our project is confirmatory and overwhelming. There are many people in the United States who have had countless experiences which they describe as the action and presence of God in their lives. These people are not restricted to a certain ethnic group, socioeconomic status or religious tradition. . . . They are not located geographically in a particular part of the country, or predominantly located in either an urban or rural setting. They are everywhere! They are your neighbors. They are you, if you will allow it.

What we saw was the validation of the phrase, *"We are one in the Spirit."*

Here were the complex mix that we call America, who the press and the media would have us believe are alienated and separated from each other, telling the same stories and having the same experiences. They came from the ghetto to the high rise, the country to the city, from the north to the south, the east to the west, and all points in between. But they were *one voice* sharing a message of hope and love and the reality of God's presence and action in each of their lives.

Did we learn anything new? In one sense, no. Scripture has informed us countless times of what we discovered in our study. What we did was to quantify and reaffirm that message through the lives and experiences of over 2,500 people living in today's world.

It is clear to us that they are truly just the tip of the iceberg!

CHAPTER 12. WHAT CAN YOU DO?

IT'S ONE THING to find convincing data that experiences of spiritual healing do indeed exist in today's world and quite another to have it happen in your life. The questions inevitably arise, "How can it happen to me?" or "How do I get it?" The questions are simple and understandable. The solutions, unfortunately, are not.

You may remember (if you are a serial reader and not a digital one) the wonderful information offered earlier in the book in the chapter entitled "Lessons and Preparations." These were suggestions by the participants in the study which came under the theme of "How do I get it?" meaning "What do I have to do to be spiritually healed; where can I go; how do I prepare myself to recognize the action of God in my life?"

Even understanding the impossibility of answering these questions with any definitive program, the suggestions are wonderful ways to focus on spiritual healing and the action of God in the world. They also reaffirm the existence of spiritual healing and the importance of centering your life in concrete ways that direct you toward God, growth, and transformation. (They are such rich and wonderful suggestions that you might want to read them again.)

Over the years of the project, we have asked ourselves the same question, knowing full well that we don't "get it" through some proscribed actions on our own initiative. As a matter of fact, it would seem that the more we try to "get it," the more it slips away, eluding our best efforts to form a plan and make it work. But the question is a persistent one and we continue to wrestle with it, just like everyone else!

The "get" part is relatively easy. How do we acquire, achieve, make happen, be in touch with something we want—sometimes desperately want? The "it" is a little more complicated, because "it" refers to the presence and/or action of God and that is something that is most accurately described as "mystery" or "miracle." So we are back to square one. How do you get/be in touch with mystery? How do you acquire a miracle? We came up with a short list from suggestions made by our participants which gives us a place to begin:

1. Asking the question is the first step.
2. Understand that God is a seeking God who wishes to love and transform you.
3. Talk to someone about it, preferably someone who has had the experience of spiritual healing.
4. There is no formula for success . . . What there is—is God!
5. Letting go is usually a part of the process: letting go of our controls.
6. The process of change is often chaotic. But that is where God dwells: out of our control.
7. You will change, but others around you may not.

Clearly, there is no path laid out here, but certain assumptions or ideas seem to underlie these reflections. Our study suggests that the process is grounded in paradox. Spiritual healing is a gift from God which is free (like grace) but which cannot be bought. In other words, you may seek it, but you cannot "get" it . . . yet it is available all the time. . . . What this means is that the process of the action and presence of God in our lives is not something we can control. The locus of control seems to be a prime issue in our understanding of this event: The control must be with God.

Time and again, we have heard stories of people desperately and faithfully trying to get God to do something for them to no avail. Finally, when they gave up and let go of their control (in these cases their insistence on some specific outcome), they suddenly experienced the presence and action of God in their life. This did not mean that their prayer specifics were granted, only that they were aware of the presence and action of God and that was enough.

What the people in our study "got" was transformed. They were changed. Their world-specific preoccupations were replaced with an experience of God's presence and a deep sense of peace. It is as if the ultimacy placed on our concerns (even the concern for God's presence) is replaced by the true ultimacy of God's presence and God's love. The experiences people have shared redefine our notions of what is true and ultimate. They are qualitatively different from our expectations and that is a transforming experience.

Some of the helpful suggestions offered by the participants in the study have included such activities as: prayer, Bible study, worship, meditation, finding a spiritual guide; reading religious texts and books; contact with others who have had such experiences. Prayer has been a particularly important activity for many of our participants. While these behaviors can be very useful, it must be noted that none of these, either singly or in combination, could be relied upon *absolutely* to achieve the goal of having an experience of God's presence or action in our life. Method may be helpful in spiritual discipline, but it does not necessarily lead to a spiritual healing or religious experience.

So, what is left? At this point, we must leave a relatively strict interpretation of our study and share some of the ideas that have come out of our experience with and our conversations about the project. A partial answer may lie in the direction of considering the ideas of *testimony, measurement and symbol, figure and ground, prayer and change.* Please understand that the following is not to be construed as some method for achieving God's presence in your life. As far as we can tell, there is no such surefire method because the process has to be under God's control, and not ours.

But these ideas may help us to predispose ourselves to a less limiting view of the problem and are drawn from our understanding of what we experienced in the project. The crazy part of it is that the gift of God's presence and action is available all the time. But we find it difficult to avail ourselves of it, to see it or to identify it for what it is. People report to us its ubiquitous nature in every corner of life. Yet it often seems far away and out of reach.

Partly, this is due to the mythology that has been built up about the action of God. It is generally presented as some incredible phenomenon (tablets of stone on a mountaintop, miracle cures, or other awesome occurrences, etc.); in other words, something unusual and on a cosmic scale! Yet we did not hear one story in the hundreds we heard that spoke of such romantic events. We suggest that this placing of God's actions on the "cosmic miracle level" is a way of trying to distance and control it. We convince ourselves that that sort of thing is not going to happen to us, so forget it! We did note, however, a number of people who, after hearing of the experiences of others, realized that they had had spiritual healing experiences themselves, but failed to identify them as such.

Generally speaking, there is a lack of vocabulary and context within the mainstream church to help people view these experiences as a normal part of spiritual development.

In order to have such a context, churches need to recognize and normalize the fact that spiritual healing does occur frequently in people's lives and provide the opportunity for them to share their experiences.

The Experience of Testimony

This points up the immense value of people sharing the stories or, to put it in a more archaic form, to *testify* or give a testimonial about their experience. We don't use these words very much any more. They seem archaic, from another time, another way to talk about religion which is old-fashioned and out of date. Or sometimes we substitute the word "witness" as in "witnessing" to one's faith. But people in the advertising profession know just how powerful "testimonials" are. They use them with great success and we buy all sorts of ordinary things based on what someone else has had to say about them.

Testimony is a remarkable experience both for the testifier and the listener. In the act of telling one's story, testifying to what has happened, the story is *reexperienced* and *revalidated*. One's heart is literally reignited! The story comes to life, not simply as a happening from the past, but rather something that is alive in the present moment as it is being shared. So much of our religious life is lived in the future, that the reality of it happening now is iconoclastic, shattering the idols of our defenses against this experience. Interestingly, for the Christian, the gospels tend to support the view that we have heard reported in our study. Jesus' interaction with people did not involve great earth-changing events in the future. People were either trans-formed at the time of the contact or they weren't. It's that simple.

For those of you who have a story to tell, we would urge you to find the courage to tell it. The sharing of these stories is such a validating experience that it places an imperative on sharing them. After all, this gift was given to you and it was made to be given away. Giving the gift to others simply increases the gift you have to give. It is clear to us that the imperative to some kind of action after the experience of spiritual healing is also a very common part of the healing process.

But any attempt to insist that these imperatives be translated into some particular action or other is simply an attempt to control the situation *ex post facto*. Listen to your heart, and not to others in these matters. Whatever form that action may take is strictly between you and God.

One of the key things that religious communities can do is to recognize the reluctance people have had to share their stories of spiritual healing and to encourage "testimony" by providing a safe and comfortable place to do so. It is relatively easy to discount many things in life, but it is difficult to discount the story you have been told by someone you know and respect.

Measurement and Symbol
Man might most aptly be called the measuring animal. Measurement is at the heart of most of our activities although we do not usually think of this as we go about our daily lives. But we measure all of our experiences all the time. Money is a ubiq-uitous measurement we all make to determine value. Value is itself a measurement of worth and so on. The object is measured as either valuable or worthless, or somewhere in between, on some scale of measurement. Our feeling states are described as

happy or unhappy. The law decides between legal and illegal acts. Medicine measures degrees of health or sickness. In order to deal with these constant and complex measurements, we ultimately rely on symbols to aid in our interpretation of life.

Symbols might be thought of as embedded equations which govern how we measure things and events. As such, they are lenses that filter out data so we can make judgments. In a sense, we are our symbols as they are the ultimate basis for our judgment about the nature of life. Different symbols produce different measurements, hence different results. They should be chosen with care, but the fact of the matter is that most of us do not know what our symbols are.

If the symbols we hold determine the measurements we make, then there is a kind of quantum aspect to the process in that measurements may be said to create the reality which we measure. Certainly, it is easy to see this in monetary terms. For instance, this bowl is three thousand years old and is worth much more than another bowl made last July (an antiquarian measurement). However, if we are making a utilitarian measurement, the July bowl is worth much more when it comes to having soup for lunch. Same object, different measurements. Reality can be said to be recreated as the symbols and their consequent measurements change.

Symbols by their nature tend to create divisions. This is worth more, this less; guilty or innocent; profitable or unprofitable; desirable or undesirable; right or wrong, and ultimately good or evil. But in relation to the presence or action of God, these divisions disappear because God is always present in every situation.

God is not sometimes present and acting and sometimes absent and not acting. God is present all the time whether we are aware of God's presence or not. One state; one pole. No divisiveness. As a symbol, it is unique. We are convinced that if you use this symbol for your measurement, your life, and the world around you, will change.

Why not consciously try to see the world through the symbol of God's presence and action in your life? Why not take a particular period of time (e.g., one month) to look at your life as being grounded in the presence and action of God and then evaluate what happens? If one tried this approach, consciously decoding one's life in this way, new ways of looking at experience would probably surface. Essentially, you are assuming the reality which you hope to find. You may not be able to define that reality, but you can point toward it and see what unfolds.

Instead of using your usual system of evaluating your experience (e.g., this is good, this other is bad), ask the question: What can this event show me about the presence or action of God in my life? How has this given event transformed my life? This represents not a method so much as a wager. You are betting some time for new insight or experience against nothing happening. Metaphorically, you are betting that God is there and cares. We are betting that that is precisely what you will find.

Figure and Ground

If you begin to see new meanings or interpretations proceed from this activity, then you might want to think of the old optical illusion of "figure and ground." This illusion consists of a design that looks like two silhouette profiles facing each other which, when your focus changes, turns into a vase. Think of the events of your life as the figure and then shift them into the ground of life as "the presence or action of God in your life." Interpret things both ways and see what happens. Seeing life in this new way may not achieve some predetermined state that you wish to have, but it will open your life to a different set of experiences and possibilities.

Will this automatically produce an experience of God as present? No, not as a guaranteed method. But it may sensitize you to seeing life in a more inclusive way, with the main ingredient being: God as present in our lives; God as action in our lives; God as the ground of our being.

Prayer

Ancillary to this is the use of prayer in relation to spiritual healing. We have found our own prayer life to have changed at a geometric rate since the project began. Before that time, our individual prayer lives were more private and relegated to times when prayer would seem to be appropriate and expected. But now prayer has become a necessary part of our living. We pray all the time—individually, together, and whenever we can we pray with others as a way to acknowledge God's continual presence in all of our lives.

Praying with another person is an act of spiritual intimacy which can have remarkable consequences. In the right circumstances, and with permission given, the time to pray is at the moment it seems appropriate, no matter where you are or what else is going on. If it seems to you that prayer is warranted, ask the person involved, and if it is all right, pray from your heart. There is never a wrong time for this kind of prayer.

We find prayer to be a critical anchor and connection. Most of the participants in the project acknowledged the importance of prayer in their healing experiences. The strongest encouragement for prayer that we found happened in our moments of prayer at each of the churches we visited. Holding hands in a gathered circle, we simply acknowledged our gratitude for presence of God and the gift of our time together. We were one body, acknowledging the gift we had received, and in that experience we were each touched and changed.

Change

In our study, some people reported to us stories and experiences which produced a moment or moments when they were clear that God was present or was acting in their lives. Other people reported the experience was cumulative. God had been acting in their lives and they suddenly realized it. Whatever the nature of your experience may have been or may come to be, we believe that one thing is certain: if you begin to look at your life as filled with the presence and action of God, and if you carry that symbol through your life, you will change.

What that change will be and where it will lead you is the mystery and the miracle of spiritual healing. All we can tell you from our experience is that if you go with the change, if you acknowledge the gift and giver of the change, and find a way to talk about what is happening in your life, the gift simply keeps growing. These activities all have the advantage of turning one's attention toward God. As our attention becomes more and more concerned with our relationship with God, the chances of our being sensitized to the presence of God are greatly increased.

As the project unfolded, people "knew" that God was continually acting in their lives, moving them in directions that brought them into more and more contact with others who also described their experiences as a "knowing." What did they "know?" How did they "know?" There was no divine messenger, no direct evidence, no religious authority assuring them that what had happened to them was the action of God in their lives. They "knew" because they were "changed," and the change was palpable, unforgettable, and indelible.

They probably didn't tell their family, friends, coworkers, or neighbors about their experience, not being sure what they would think. They surely didn't look different physically. They may not have acted in a different way. They probably didn't appear more religious. But they were different internally, and that difference had to do with their spirit. Their spirit was ignited and in that process they felt healed.

Our healing was a felt "connection" to God, and a "knowing" that God had somehow mysteriously entered our lives and changed them. This amazing group of randomly selected, geographically, ethnically, and socioeconomically diverse people; black and white; male and female; rich and poor; young and old; educated and not educated; from the country and the city had all responded to the question, "What is Spiritual Healing?"

We had raised that question 116 times and the answer was absolutely clear: Spiritual healing is the action and/or presence of God in our lives. Spiritual healing is a change of state in us that is recognizable and permanent. Spiritual healing is an experience of the peace of God.

We expected to bring you facts—results and conclusions based on our research findings—which we did. But, we also bring you the mystery and miracle that we experienced in doing the project because it has changed our lives and because it is the greatest gift that we have ever experienced. We have also learned that gifts received must be shared, for such is the true nature of gifts from God:

*Spiritual healing is a gift which you can't "get,"
but which you can have. And when you have it,
you must give it away. You must share it!*

The biggest obstacle to spiritual healing is ourselves. We stand in the way of God's actions again and again as we insist (however rationally) that we are the best judge of what should happen. As we do this we become "blind" and "deaf" to the action of God.

Jesus spent a great deal of time addressing the problem of the deaf and the blind. Certainly, few really "saw" him as God acting in the world or "heard" what he had to say. Things haven't changed much, but the divine potential of God's presence and action is everywhere, all the time, as it always has been. That potential stands ready to transform you at any moment if you will allow it.

We encourage you to take the risk of looking at your own life through these new (and yet very old) symbols and to see what happens when you focus your attention on God and God's loving presence in this world. We lovingly challenge you to share your own words and stories about God with another person or persons and in so doing experience the gift of "testimony." Testimony validates the action of God in your life for others and in that same action it revalidates it for you.

We offer you the amazing opportunity of sharing your experience with others who need to hear your words and stories in order that they might discover their own! This is how the gift of God's presence and love continues to be alive in our midst today: through an ongoing, multifaceted, diverse company of ordinary people who are learning to see life as an amazing and surprising adventure and who are creating a modern-day "Gospel According to the People," with their lives.

We invite you to engage in a process that might be called "God talk": conversations about the presence or action of God in your life with family, friends, people at church, maybe even at work. "God Talk" is a reminder that God is present in everything that we do and is continually trying to attract our attention by the amazing gifts that God offers. Recognizing and naming those gifts is "God talk."

But if you don't feel quite ready to engage in your own personal "God talk," then this book offers you the opportunity to tell the story of the Spiritual Healing Project to others. It gives you an easy entry to the whole subject, without risking your own experience. We think you may be surprised at how many people have a story to tell you, once you've given them the chance.

Finally, as one person put it to us in a voice that rang with simplicity and truth:

Just do it!

Turn your attention to God.

Look at your life as filled with the action and presence of God.

Pray a lot.

Tell your story.

Just do it!

And see what happens.

And we say:

Amen!

Rev. Bobbie McKay, Ph.D., and Lewis A. Musil, M.A.

CHAPTER 13. OUR INDIVIDUAL EXPERIENCES WITH THE PROJECT

THE SPIRITUAL HEALING Project has touched and trans-formed our lives, both collectively and individually. We have experienced the full measure of words and stories, tears and joys, mysteries and miracles expressed by over 2,500 people. As they shared their stories about the action and presence of God in their lives, we wanted to share each of our personal responses to the project, for we are as changed as they are.

Their story has become our story as well.

From Lew:

When Bobbie first told me of her ideas about the Spiritual Healing Project, I was naturally receptive because I knew her ideas are always worth listening to, especially ideas that have to do with theological matters. We have been blessed with a mutual interest in these things, so I listened.

What I did not realize was that that was what I would do all through the project: listen. Do not misunderstand, I provided plenty of input throughout (such is the nature of our relation-ship). But my job was to be the scribe . . . to listen and write down what I heard. It was not an easy job. But, fortunately, I had a good ear for people's speech and ideas from my early life in theater and television, and I made out all right.

I did not know what I thought we would find in the project. But one thing I found right away was the number of surprise gifts that God had in store for us. The first one was the size of the project. We had envisioned a twenty to twenty-five church sample because we had decided to fund this project ourselves. We figured that we could somehow scrape up the money to do that many churches, but when we had a response of ninety six churches and the almost immediate addition of six more, we were in a different ball game, financially and in every other way.

We were in agreement. We could not say "no" to any of them. We took the plunge, and what a swim it was!

I think back over that experience in wonder and awe as a jumble of church basements, sanctuaries, meeting rooms, parsonages, of little struggling churches and summer heat and big, successful churches and catching planes, motel rooms, long drives in bad weather, but these things pale before what my ears picked up in one meeting after another.

For I sat down with people 116 times from every conceivable walk and condition of life and they told me stories: stories of their travels with God. And we became fellow travelers in those moments in ways that would have been denied us in normal society. Everywhere, I was at home in the Spirit with everyone. There was no color, language, socioeconomic, or political barrier present. We were one. We were one in the Spirit! There was no fear or envy or prejudice . . . only people telling how God acted in their lives.

At first, I didn't know quite what to think. I tried to make some sense out of my experiences and explain them with varying results. But, I was unaware of the cumulative effect of the experiences. They were to be life-changing.

Slowly, I began to see an emerging picture of America and Americans that was entirely different from the one nightly painted on the tube. Instead of a world of division and violence, of moral bankruptcy and hedonism, I found wise people from all walks of life who were kind and decent and not the victims of society and history that were paraded nightly on the media. These were people of spirit and they were everywhere. They were not a moral majority. They were a spiritual plurality who were transformed and transforming. No one remarked them because they were the fabric of life, not the designs of society. They were so present everywhere that they were invisible.

And I came to know that God is alive in this world through his people and that he, too, seemed invisible because he was omnipresent. It was like living in two worlds that shifted and morphed into each other. Which was the real world? Both were, but the world of spirit was both fundamental and transcendent. There was, however, one more step for me to go.

I listened to the stories and I knew they were true. But I could not claim a story for myself. It would be almost three and a half years of listening and thinking before I had a story of my own to tell.

On the night before this past Christmas, I was about as low as a snake's belt buckle. I had particularly resolved to have Christmas happen that year . . . really happen . . . to get beyond the hype and the veneer and really penetrate the inside of that incredible birth. I had gotten about as close to the experience as I had to my first space mission flight and time was running out.

We had been to some celebrations in the recent past which were marked out by noise, cigarette smoke, and general disconnect from the season, and my mood was closer to Attila the Hun than Father Christmas. Late that Christmas Eve, my take on Christmas was grim. I felt deprived of Christmas and I was particularly lumpy and unhelpful to Bobbie.

I went to bed without so much as a Ho-Ho-Ho and awoke the next morning in, if possible, a worse state than I had left the night before. It was Christmas, but it was not Christmas, not anywhere near Christmas. We had to busy ourselves for an early Christmas church service which was being held at our home. It was my last hope to salvage something.

Then, during our morning prayers, I decided to simplify things and simply pray for God's will. Big mistake! I had left out of my prayer much material which I normally included and which I thought was inconsistent with my attempt to simplify and salvage what was left of Christmas.

My dear wife did not appreciate my simplification and felt that my omissions showed a want of caring and general disregard. At this point, I lost it. I suddenly felt that I had not only missed Christmas, but that I had made some fatal and irrevocable error in my relationship with my wife and everything else. I quite honestly sobbed the sob of the lost. And then Bobbie said to me, "Wait! Lew! Those last couple of days . . . that was Bethlehem!"

And I stopped, transfixed. Of course, she was right. That was Bethlehem . . . noisy and crowded . . . full of people who did not want to be there . . . a birth in a stable . . . a baby lying in the feeding trough. And suddenly, I gave birth to Christmas. The presence of the God who came into the world was born one more time and it required my labor and my pain and it was the gift that transcended all gifts.

It was my first Christmas. I was sixty-nine years old and I remember it like it was yesterday.

I hope that our travels with God will give you the gifts we have seen so many times.

From Bobbie:

The Spiritual Healing Project has been the culmination of a wondrous experience that began with my conversion thirty-five years ago. At that time, I learned that God mysteriously acts in ways that seem to turn our lives upside down and inside out, propelling us in new and unexpected directions—if we are willing to go along with God's gifts and plans. God is the great initiator of surprises! Like fireworks on the fourth of July, they dazzle us with their explosive and unfolding brilliance. What can we say but "Oh" or "Ah" or "Wow"!

So it has been with the project. From the moment of its conception to these final days of completion, the project has been filled with gifts and surprises, all of them unexpected and unplanned. Each successive step has moved the project along with an ease that was simply marvelous to behold. One is reminded of the words, "My yoke is easy and my burden is light," for such was the essential nature of our experience in doing the project.

Certainly, there were tight places along the way, particularly as we were fitting extensive travels into limited schedules. Finding our way in unfamiliar territory became Lew's job (sometimes nightmare), while I navigated, struggling to read maps with print too small to read and directions that didn't always make sense. Only once in our 116 visits did we have to cancel a meeting and that was only because I got sick and we couldn't catch our flight.

But overriding any of the problems we encountered was the constant sense of excitement we experienced which kept us in our own state of "Oh," "Ah," and "Wow"! Each new church was a new gift of people, words, and stories that became the anchor of who we were becoming. Lew and I have always been people of faith, Christians who strongly believe in the truth of the gospels. But the project brought our faith to life in a new and unexpected way. You cannot hear the voices of over 2,500 people raised in story and praise without being utterly changed. And changed we were!

The first change I noticed in myself was watching Scripture come to life. The words from Matthew (18:20), "Where two or three are gathered in my name, there am I in the midst of them," simply became the life-giving theme for all our meetings. We always felt that God was present. God was there each time we prayed; each time a word or story was shared; each moment of silence; each time of tears. God was there when we held hands to pray or spontaneously hugged each other at the close of our time together. God was there in the release and relief of words long held in silent remembrance. God was there in the depth of the mystery that each healing reflected.

The scripture from Luke describing Jesus' ministry to the brokenhearted, the captives, the blind, and the bruised (4:18) were universal words which reached deep into the heart and soul of those who came to the project. For each of them, the presence of God was part of their lives today. Their own words and stories of healing were creating a new gospel built around a very old theme: God's love for us and God's wish to be with us: all of us with no exceptions, and for all time.

As time went on, it became clear that doing our project was the most important thing we were doing with our lives. Although each of us was engaged in other pursuits, this was the centering part of who we were. And it grew in giftedness! Each church and temple provided us with new insights into the action of God. Each person's story brought us closer to the real truths of life. We found ourselves filled with a spirit that kept us moving and growing.

We'd started out thinking we would collect some words, hear a few stories, and document our experience in some way. We had no idea of the door we were opening and the riches we would find. We had indeed discovered a "pearl of great price" in a field that had come to life for both of us. Having discovered that great gift, we could do nothing less than pursue the unfolding of whatever surprises God had in store for us, wherever they take us, for whatever amount of time is necessary.

From the beginning, I understood that this was God's project. Whatever I did felt like necessary actions for the unfolding of the project, the "making it happen" part. That included both the sacred experiences of doing the project, and the more mundane times of typing letters, making phone calls, scheduling churches and airplanes; packing, running, planning, paying attention to endless details to fit everything in.

But the person in charge, the CEO of the whole operation, was God, and when God is in charge, everything has a "rightness" about it. It's not trouble-free by any means. But there is a transcendent sense that this is the core of what it means to be in relationship with God: God in charge, and us trying to be wise enough to figure out what to do, but knowing fully where the credit belongs.

We experienced some specific changes in the way we live our lives. We started to pray before each meal, including times when we were in restaurants. This was not done in an ostentatious way, but rather it felt like a necessary way to be in connection with God on a regular basis. It became a necessity, not a choice. We needed a time to be thankful. But at one of our meals, a waitress noticed our praying and commented enthusiastically, "Hey, that was really cool what you guys were doing!" She's right! It is pretty cool to acknowledge the living presence of God and be thankful.

We hung a large map of the United States on a wall near the kitchen with a good-sized dot marking each of the cities we had visited. It is an impressive and visible reminder of just how far we had traveled and how many churches we had visited. I pass it several times a day. Each time, I marvel at how it changed our lives; I wonder how we ever managed to do it and then I remember that we didn't do it alone, and I am filled with gratitude.

Our grandchildren refer to the project as "Gramma's crazy mission." I like that title because when you get involved with God it sometimes feels a little crazy. God does not lead us down familiar paths that are "politically correct." In fact, some of God's gifts present unique and unusual opportunities that are definitely off the mainstream of life. Sometimes the "wow" of surprises contains a few 'ouches" along the way. But it is clear that God's call has brought each of us into a fuller and richer life than we could ever have imagined or planned ourselves. That is sufficient.

The added bonus of our new life has been the privilege of meeting so many people whose lives have directly gifted ours. Their words and stories were constant reminders of the presence of God in this world. Their openness and eagerness to share their lives was a tangible welcome that said, without words, "We're glad you're here, and we hope you'll not hurry away too quickly. Linger a while and get to know us." Their tears were direct evidence of their trust and faith, the great gift that always says" "Pay attention! These are words of life and truth."

As our individual lives have been enriched and changed by the project, so has our relationship. We've always enjoyed a deep and loving relationship that revolved around our children, our careers, and our church commitment. We've loved talking "theology" and we knew that God was really the center of our lives. But like so many people, we were too busy; we had too many obligations, too many needs, too much to do, and too little time. The God-centered part of our lives was always having to shift to the periphery to accommodate the demands that life seemed to impose on us.

The project became the linchpin that pulled all the pieces back to the center. Once our commitment was made to follow God's plan to the fullest, with no reservations as to cost or time, our "other" lives began to form the outer spaces, leaving a marvelous center filled with the living presence of God. Our separate lives now had a common "home," a place where we were united with God and with each other. The gifts we each brought to our relationship were now drawn together into a unified theme of gratitude and thanksgiving.

Our own healing was the gift we had never expected to receive. The "peace" that so many had described became our "peace." Our commitment to continuing the project, beyond its original plan, has become the central part of our lives. We decided to express this decision in a covenant to spend the remainder of our lives bringing the words and stories of God's healing presence to others. In whatever form the project now takes, in whatever way we can, we will continue the work. Wherever God leads us, we will follow!

The final gift of the project came as mysteriously as the first gift. Just as my own conversion experience set the stage for all that was to come, it was in Lew's conversion experience, a few months ago, that we felt the project pulling us even more deeply into the mystery and presence of God. To know that God has acted directly in our lives and the lives of others is to know that God does act and that God will continue to act. The Spiritual Healing Project has brought those words to life for us. We pray that they may open that door for you as well. Praise God!

CHAPTER 14. THE GIFT OF THE UNEXPECTED GIFTS

FROM THE BEGINNING, the Spiritual Healing Project revealed the "gift of the unexpected gift," the gift you do not plan or control but which unfolds when God is present in your life. For us, everything about the project was unexpected and therefore a gift that surpassed all imagined or sought outcomes. The unexpected gift takes you by surprise and leads you into new territory with new possibilities, new roads to be taken, and new discoveries to be made, all of which become life-changing!

Our unexpected gifts began with the original sense of calling to discover the meaning of those mysterious words, "spiritual healing." Then came the gifts of the design, the sample, and the amazing response we received to our invitation to engage in spiritual intimacy with two strangers.

The gifts continued to unfold as naturally as a seed planted in rich soil and nourished by care and attention, producing a garden of color, texture, and beauty—surely a familiar story. Our meeting with 101 Protestant churches produced over two thousand new gifts. The unexpected addition of our Catholic churches brought a new dimension to our study, filling it with more gifts. Bringing the Jewish community into our study brought us into the very foundation of our religious tradition, powerfully rooting us in our Judeo-Christian heritage, a history filled with gifts.

The words and stories we were given were all precious gifts of the heart and spirit, many told for the first time, and each one a significant and special contribution to our work. The entire project became an unexpected gift of "oneness":

- the "oneness" of words spoken, and particularly the one word used by each tradition to describe spiritual healing: "peace," the "peace of God," the transformed moment.
- the "oneness" of stories told, filled with the themes of God present and active in each person's life: the never-to-be-forgotten benchmark of spiritual birth.
- the "oneness" of depth and mystery, tears shared and stories told for the first time.

One of the most unexpected gifts of the project was the gift of the presence of God at each meeting and the sense of healing that occurred in our time together: healing unsought, but clearly given. Out of this unexpected healing came a sense of transformation which infused the group with a new spirit.

The gift of our own transformation brought us into a brand-new sense of calling and mission. We had unexpectedly become "missionaries," with a lifetime commitment to bringing the "story" of the project to all who would listen.

The unexpected and universal gift of "community" has become the most powerful gift we have received in the project. In this simple, wondrous action of telling our stories about God to each other, all barriers between us disappear. There are no ethnic, creedal, socioeconomic, geographic, or gender differences when we share the presence or action of God in our lives. We become a universal community bound by our connections to God and to each other. It creates the possibilities for an interfaith experience among very diverse people and the opportunity for dialogue and peace between us. What greater gift could we discover!

When we began our journey six years ago, we had expected to be two people traveling together to gather data for a research project. But one, as one usually turns out to be, would be wrong! What started out as an attempt to answer a simple question turned into a life-changing experience for both of us. And that experience was a total surprise: an unexpected gift.

In our planning and scraping and doing . . . in the rush for planes, motel food, and long drives . . . in the remarkable experience of participating in the spiritual journeys of others, we became aware that we were not traveling alone. There was always another passenger with us, not just along for the ride, but shaping and changing us in ways we could not imagine, and who turned out to be the best traveling companion we could ever have.

We would invite you to look at your own journey and see, if indeed you have not already seen, the same loving companion traveling with you!

Have a surprising journey!

Bobbie McKay and Lew Musil

Rev. Bobbie McKay, Ph.D., and Lewis A. Musil, M.A.

AUTHORS' CREDENTIALS:

Reverend Bobbie McKay, Ph.D., is a licensed clinical psychologist and an ordained minister in the United Church of Christ. Dr. McKay has been engaged in both of these helping/healing professions for almost thirty years. She is the author of two books published by Pilgrim Press: *The Unabridged Woman: A Guide to Growing Up Female*, and *Whatever Happened to the Family: A Psychologist Looks at Sixty Years of Change*, as well as numerous articles about children, families, marriage, and spiritual growth. She has led over eight hundred workshops and seminars regarding psychological and spiritual health and has appeared on both television and radio.

Lewis A. Musil holds a bachelor's degree from the University of Chicago and a Master of Fine Arts degree from the Art Institute, Chicago, Illinois. Mr. Musil has been a writer, producer, and director of theater and television for thirty-five years. He was awarded a grant from the Field Foundation for an innovative theater project on Chicago's west side. He has taught extensively. He was Visiting Professor in the area of Religion and the Arts at Garrett Theological Seminary. He has also taught at Elmhurst College and the Goodman Theater School of the Art Institute. He was chairman of the Department of Creative Drama in the Evanston Public Schools for sixteen years. Dr. McKay and Mr. Musil are married and live in Wilmette, Illinois. They have four children and nine grandchildren.

THE CHURCHES IN THE SPIRITUAL HEALING PROJECT

The Participating Churches from the United Church of Christ:

First Congregational Church	Binghamton, New York
Shepherd of the Hills Church	Laguna Niguel California
First Congregational Church	South Hadley, Massachusetts
St. Mark's United Church of Christ	Baltimore, Maryland
Plymouth Congregational Church	Louisville, Kentucky
First Congregational Church	Santa Cruz, California
Zion United Church of Christ	Le Sueur, Minnesota
Faith United Church of Christ	Cleveland, Ohio
Church of the Beatitudes	Phoenix, Arizona
First Congregational Church	Ada, Michigan
Faith United Church	State College, Pennsylvania
Park Hill Congregational Church	Denver, Colorado
United Church of Sun City	Sun City, Arizona
Heritage United Church of Christ	Baltimore, Maryland
Bear Creek Church	Eagle Butte, South Dakota
United Church of Los Alamos	Los Alamos, New Mexico
First Congregational Church	Flagstaff, Arizona
Lakeville United Church of Christ	Lakeville, New York
The Old South Church	Boston, Massachusetts
United Church of Christ	Lake Oswego, Oregon
Immanuel Congregational Church	Hartford, Connecticut

United Church of Christ	Maquoketa, Iowa
Second Congregational Church	Rockford, Illinois
Howland Congregational Church	Warren, Ohio
Congregational Church	Danville, California
First Congregational Church	Eugene, Oregon
First Church of Christ	Springfield, Massachusetts
Church of the Open Door	Miami, Florida
Mayflower Community Church	Minneapolis, Minnesota
Central Congregational Church	Atlanta, Georgia
St. John's United Church of Christ	Newport, Kentucky
First Parish Congregational Church	Yarmouth, Maine
First Congregational Church	North Adams, Massachusetts
Hampshire Colony Congregational	Princeton, Illinois
First Congregational Church	Ithaca, New York
Woodfords Congregational Church	Portland, Maine
St. Stephen Church	Greensboro, North Carolina
Pilgrim Congregational Church	Cleveland, Ohio
Church of the Apostles	Lancaster, Pennsylvania
First Congregational Church	Clinton, Iowa
Central Congregational Church	Dallas, Texas
First Congregational Church	Canandaigua, New York
Congregational United Church	Claremont, California
Plymouth Congregational Church	Des Moines, Iowa
St. Paul's United Church of Christ	Chicago, Illinois
Immanuel/Ferguson United Church	St. Louis, Missouri
Congregational Church	Algonquin, Illinois
First Congregational Church	Traverse City, Michigan
Church of Park Manor	Chicago, Illinois
West Side United Church of Christ	Cleveland, Ohio
Parliview Congregational Church	Aurora, Colorado
St. Peter's Church	South Bead, Indiana
First Parish Church	Brunswick, Maine,
First Congregational Church	Concord, New Hampshire

First Congregational Church	La Crosse, Wisconsin
Circular Congregational Church	Charleston, South Carolina
Congregational Church	West Newbury, Vermont
St. Peter's Pleasant Ridge Church	Cincinnati, Ohio
First Congregational Church	Madison, Wisconsin
Bethany United Church of Christ	Baltimore, Maryland
St. John's Church	Kullman Alabama
Salem United Church of Christ	Rochester, Now York
St. Paul's Church	Pottstown, Pennsylvania
Salem United Church of Christ	Doylestown, Pennsylvania
United Church of Christ	Peshastin, Washington
First United Church of Christ	Tipton, Iowa
Plymouth Congregational Church	Lawrence, Kansas
First Congregational Church	Boulder, Colorado
First Congregational Church	Muskegon, Michigan
First Congregational Church	Appleton, Wisconsin
Philippine United Church of Christ	Chicago, Illinois
Central Congregational Church	Topeka, Kansas
First Congregational Church	Chicago, Illinois
Community Church of Vero Beach	Vero Beach, Florida
First Congregational Church	Marietta, Ohio
San Lucas Church	Chicago, Illinois
Plymouth Congregational Church	Seattle, Washington
Christ Church	Evansville, Indiana
Grace United Church of Christ	Baltimore, Maryland
Morningside Congregational Church	Inglewood, California
Brookmeade Congregational Church	Nashville, Tennessee
Bethel/Freelandville Church	Edwardsport, Indiana
Peace United Church of Christ	Rochester, Minnesota
Community Church of Mill 'Valley	Mill Valley, California
Church of Peace	Fond du Lac, Wisconsin
The Foreside Community Church	Falmouth, Maine
St. Albans Congregational Church	St. Albans, New York

Ainsworth United Church of Christ	Portland, Oregon
Congregational United Church	Belmont, California
Congregational Church of Hollis	Hollis, New Hampshire
Pilgrim United Church of Christ	Los Angeles, California
Barre Congregational Church	Barre, Vermont
Kensington United Church of Christ	Kensington, Connecticut
Centre Congregational Church	Brattleboro, Vermont
Colonial Park United Church	Harrisburg, Pennsylvania
First Congregational United Church	Westfield, New Jersey
Bethlehem United Church of Christ	Ann Arbor, Michigan
First Plymouth Congregational	Lincoln, Nebraska
First Congregational Church	Barstow, California
Christ Church United	Dracut, Massachusetts

The Participating Catholic Churches

Saint Ailbee	Chicago, Illinois
Queen of All Saints	Chicago, Illinois
Saint Mary of the Woods	Chicago, Illinois
Saint Lake	River Forest, Illinois
Saint Benedict the African	Chicago, Illinois (West)
Our Lady of Mt. Carmel	Chicago, Illinois
Saint Joseph	Wilmette, Illinois
Saint Hyacinth	Chicago, Illinois
Old Saint Pat's	Chicago, Illinois
Saint Agnes Church	Chicago Heights, Illinois
Infant of Prague Church	Flossmoor, Illinois

The Participating Jewish Congregations

Temple B'nai Jehoshua Beth Elohim	Glenview, Illinois
Beth Tikvah Congregation	Hoffman Estates, Illinois
Beth Emet: The Free Synagogue	Evanston, Illinois
Moses Montefiore Congregation	Bloomington, Illinois